The Irish Diaspora

The Irish Diaspora

John Gibney (ed.)

PEN & SWORD HISTORY

AN IMPRINT OF PEN & SWORD BOOKS LTD.
YORKSHIRE – PHILADELPHIA

First published in Great Britain in 2020 by
Pen And Sword History
An imprint of
Pen & Sword Books Ltd
Yorkshire – Philadelphia

Produced in association with *History Ireland*: www.historyireland.com

Hardback ISBN: 9781526736833
Paperback ISBN: 9781526769572

The right of John Gibney to be identified as Editor of this work has been asserted by him in accordance with the Copyright, Designs and Patents Act 1988.

A CIP catalogue record for this book is available from the British Library.

Typeset by Aura Technology and Software Services, India.
Printed and bound in the UK by TJ International

Pen & Sword Books Ltd incorporates the Imprints of Pen & Sword Books Archaeology, Atlas, Aviation, Battleground, Discovery, Family History, History, Maritime, Military, Naval, Politics, Railways, Select, Transport, True Crime, Fiction, Frontline Books, Leo Cooper, Praetorian Press, Seaforth Publishing, Wharncliffe and White Owl.

For a complete list of Pen & Sword titles please contact

PEN & SWORD BOOKS LIMITED
47 Church Street, Barnsley, South Yorkshire, S70 2AS, England
E-mail: enquiries@pen-and-sword.co.uk
Website: www.pen-and-sword.co.uk

or

PEN AND SWORD BOOKS
1950 Lawrence Rd, Havertown, PA 19083, USA
E-mail: Uspen-and-sword@casematepublishers.com
Website: www.penandswordbooks.com

Contents

Preface

Ireland is known worldwide as a country that produces emigrants. The existence of the Irish 'diaspora' is the subject of this fifth instalment of the 'Irish perspectives' collaboration between Pen and Sword and *History Ireland*. From the early Christian era Irish missionaries travelled across Europe; from the early modern period Irish soldiers served across the world in various European armies and empires; and in the modern era, Ireland's position on the edge of the Atlantic made Irish emigrants amongst the most visible migrants in an era of mass migration. Ranging from Europe to Africa to the Americas and Australia, this anthology explores the lives and experiences of Irish educators, missionaries, soldiers and insurgents, from those who simply sought a better life overseas to those with little choice in the matter, and who established an Irish presence across the globe as they did so.

The chapters below have all been drawn from the archives of *History Ireland*, and re-edited; with regards to illustrations, every effort has been made to contact rights holders. If we have missed any, the error will be rectified in any subsequent edition.

Contributors

Michael Doorley is the author of *Irish-American diaspora nationalism: the Friends of Irish Freedom, 1916–1935* (Four Courts Press, 2005).

Patrick Fitzgerald is Lecturer and Development Officer at the Mellon Centre for Migration Studies at the Ulster American Folk Park.

The late David Fitzpatrick was Emeritus Professor of History at Trinity College Dublin.

John Gibney is a historian with the Royal Irish Academy's Documents on Irish Foreign Policy series.

James McConnel is Associate Professor in History at Northumbria University.

Kerby A. Miller is Emeritus Professor of History at the University of Missouri.

Hiram Morgan is Senior Lecturer in History at University College Cork.

Oscar Recio Morales completed his Ph.D in History at the University of Alcala.

Edmundo Murray is the author of *Becoming Irlandés: Private Narratives of the Irish Emigration to Argentina (1844–1912)* (Buenos Aires, 2012).

Theresa Denise Murray is a graduate of University College Cork.

Rachel Naylor is a Research Associate of Ulster University.

Máirtín Ó Catháin is Lecturer in History at the University of Central Lancashire.

Aidan O'Hara is an award-winning broadcaster, writer, and historian.

Joe Regan completed his Ph.D in history at NUI Galway.

Dagmar Ó Riain-Raedel formerly lectured in history at University College Cork.

Nini Rodgers is an Honorary Senior Research Fellow in the School of History, Anthropology, Philosophy and Politics, Queen's University, Belfast.

David A. Wilson is Professor of History at the University of Toronto.

Barbara Walsh completed her Ph.D in History at Lancaster University.

Introduction

Irish Diasporas

John Gibney

One of the most well-known facts about the history of Ireland and its peoples is that, throughout recorded history, large numbers of those people have left the island on which they were born to work or settle overseas. The existence of the so-called 'Irish Diaspora' is perhaps to be expected, given Ireland's relatively small size and its location on the Atlantic seaboard of Europe. People have moved back and forth from the island of Ireland for centuries; the essays collected here explore some aspects of the history of those who left Ireland, rather then those who arrived there, over the centuries.

There are, of course, as many reasons for emigrating as there are emigrants. In the early Christian era, Irish monasteries became centres of learning after the fall of the Roman Empire, and their clergy played a major role in exporting Christianity back to the Continent in the early Middle Ages. Even aside from the cultural and religious bonds that this fostered (as reflected in the experience of the pilgrims described by Dagmar Ó Riain-Raedel), other seemingly universal phenomena attracted the interest of the Irish: the Irish military diasporas of the early modern era can be seen, in part, as a response to upheaval and conquest at home (though the experience of the inhabitants of Baltimore, as explored here by Denise Therese Murray, was an upheaval of a very different kind). By the eighteenth century Continental Europe had a network of Irish colleges and the armies of many of its countries had a tradition of Irish military service; Irish mercantile families were ensconced in many of the trading ports of France (some of whom, as Nini Rodgers reveals, were involved in the Atlantic slave trade). In the early eighteenth century much of this arose from the Catholic and Jacobite diaspora who emigrated after the Williamite victory of 1691 (the so-called 'Wild Geese'). Looking across the Atlantic, an Irish Presbyterian diaspora began to emerge in North America (as explored by Patrick Fitzgerald). And over time, ideas and ideology could emigrate as much as people, from the republicanism of the United Irishmen and the Fenians to the popular loyalism of the Orange Order.

Yet the emigrant flow from Ireland during the nineteenth century overshadows its various predecessors, as between 1801 and 1921 perhaps as many as eight million people emigrated from Ireland. Even before the Great Famine of the

1840s (often, and understandably, assumed to be the pivotal moment for mass emigration in the Victorian era) the Irish were a major source of overseas labour in Britain and North America. Indeed, New York eventually had more Irish-born residents than Dublin by the middle of the century, with districts such as Five Points (depicted in Martin Scorsese's 2002 epic *Gangs of New York*) and institutions like Tamanny Hall, the headquarters of the Democratic Party in the city, becoming dominated by the Irish. The Irish language also became part of the vernacular of the American cities to which the Irish flocked, though its cultural legacy in American idiom remains unclear and contested.

The enormous level of emigration witnessed during the famine was never repeated, but it opened the door to mass emigration throughout the second half of the nineteenth century and up to the eve of the First World War. As well as creating new communities in North *and* South America (the latter phenomenon is explored by Edmundo Murray), emigration also had a legacy at home by facilitating the remoulding of Ireland's social structures; with the dispersal of so many of the 'have-nots', both male and female, the Irish population declined at a remarkable and steady rate after the famine. Mass emigration was perhaps the single most important driver of change at all levels of Irish society in the Victorian era, as emigration whittled away at the numbers living on the island.

Irish emigrants did not just move to the Americas, for amongst the Irish diaspora must be counted the thousands of Irish who peopled both the British empire, its structures, and indeed the military that had obtained it. In 1830 nearly 43% of the British army were Irish, while Ireland made up just over 32% of the UK population, and remained very visible wherever it went; the eponymous hero of Rudyard Kipling's famous novel *Kim* (1901) was the son of an Irish soldier. And many of the new Indian Civil Service that, in the second half of the century, made up the bureaucracy of the Raj were Irish, both Protestant and Catholic. Catholic (and, to a much lesser degree, Protestant) missionary activity also took place under the auspices of the empire. In other words, alongside the understandable and justified image of the Irish ending up around the world almost as exiles–victims of British misgovernment–mention must be made of those Irish who administered and fought for the empire itself.

On the other hand, diaspora communities offered vital support and experience to organisations dedicated to freeing Ireland from British rule. The importance of the diaspora was to be seen during the revolutionary period of the early twentieth century, as shown here by Michael Doorley. Mobilising the diaspora in the US and was a key strategy of the independence movement, in terms of raising its profile and obtaining funding and weapons. Indeed, groups like the IRA organised extensively within Irish communities in Britain and carried out attacks there.

Emigration was often held up as the proof of British misrule. But the transition to independence did not bring it to an end. In 1931 one in every four Irish-born people lived overseas, and from the 1930s onwards the major destination for emigrants became Britain rather than the US, a reality strengthened by post–Second World War reconstruction. And even aside from the economic imperative, the bright lights of British cities offered an attractive alternative to young men and women from what was still a conservative society. As the links to the US weakened in the twentieth century, that to the UK remained paradoxically strong.

That said, the emigrant flow and the emergence of the diaspora communities generally ebbed and flowed according to economic conditions. The economic boom of the late twentieth and early twenty-first century saw the Irish emigrant flow reverse as immigration became a major phenomenon (there are many other countries whose various diasporas are now represented in Ireland). The pendulum swung back with the financial crisis of 2008, as emigration began again; this is a sign, perhaps, that it will always be a feature of Irish life, especially in the traditional destinations of North America, Britain, and Australasia. The chapters that follow point towards the lived experience of at least some of those Irish people – and their descendants – who, over the centuries, for whatever reason and for however long, made the journey outward from their homeland.

Chapter 1

The Irish medieval pilgrimage to Santiago de Compostela

Dagmar Ó Riain-Raedel

In October 1996 the foundations of what is thought to have been the thirteenth-century Augustinian priory of St Mary were located during building work for a new shopping centre at Mullingar, County Westmeath. During the archaeological rescue excavation under the direction of Michael Gibbons, more than thirty burials were discovered, two of which contained scallop shells, one of them in combination with a bone relic. Exactly ten years earlier, similar finds of scallop shells had been made by Miriam Clyne during excavations at St Mary's Cathedral, Tuam, County Galway, probably, as in Mullingar, also of thirteenth/fourteenth century origin. An exciting discovery was made by Fionnbarr Moore in 1992 underneath the wall of a late medieval tomb at Ardfert Cathedral. He found a pewter scallop shell, on which a little bronze-gilded figure of St James had been mounted. The shell was attached to a brooch, clearly defining it as a pilgrim's badge. The emblem of the shell has always been connected with the apostle James (*Jacobus maior*) and its occurrence in a burial usually indicates that the deceased had been a pilgrim to the grave of the apostle in Santiago (*Sant'Iago* i.e., St James) de Compostela in Northern Spain. The twelfth-century *Liber Sancti Jacobi* mentions stalls selling scallop shells in the proximity of the cathedral at Santiago, and states that returning pilgrims carried these with them, just as Jerusalem pilgrims carried palm-leaves. Fortunately for us, while the palms may not have survived, some of the scallop shells did, thus providing some indication of the extent of the Irish involvement in one of the great pilgrimages of Europe.

The emergence of the cult of St James is not easily reconstructed. It seems, however, that the missionary activities of this disciple of Christ's, before his martyrdom in Palestine in 42AD, as recorded in the Acts of the Apostles, were greatly amplified in the following centuries. The mission of St James was now said to have extended to Spain and by the ninth century, martyrologies refer to the translation of the body of St James to Galicia. In conjunction with this development, the apostle now also began to assume the role of patron of Spain, and when the northern Spanish episcopate, in co-operation with

1. The cathedral at Santiago de Compostela.

the kings of Asturias and Galicia, rediscovered there the long-forgotten tomb of St James, the spectacular rise of Santiago was assured. St James' alleged missionary activities in Spain were now increasingly a source of inspiration in the ongoing fight against the Moors. Moreover, custody of the apostle's burial place was utilised to great advantage by the northern kings who were claiming powers similar to those held by the Visigothic hierarchy of the south. The outcome was the establishment of an episcopal, and later archiepiscopal, see at Santiago.

Yet the popularity of the pilgrimage to Santiago, rivalling that of Jerusalem and Rome, would never have come about, had it not been for a series of circumstances dating to the tenth and eleventh centuries. By this time, the Spanish kingdoms on their side of the Pyrenees had forged close alliances with their counterparts in France, and particularly so with the authorities in Aquitaine and Burgundy. It was in fact French interest in promoting, and protecting, the routes leading from France into Spain, that first opened up the possibility of visiting the shrine at Santiago in relative safety. The powerful Burgundian abbey of Cluny, in particular, established and controlled numerous monasteries along the pilgrims' routes and aristocratic families on both sides of the Pyrenees followed this example with foundations of their own. These also established *hospitia* and assumed responsibility for the general upkeep of the route.

The eleventh century generally was also a time when travel in Europe, hazardous during the invasions of Vikings, Saracens and Magyars, became widely possible again. Pilgrimages to all kinds of shrines were now undertaken with renewed effort. In these more peaceful circumstances the abbey of Cluny began eagerly to promote pilgrimages to as far afield as Jerusalem and Santiago. And it was the Cluniac message of the 'overriding importance of the remission of sins' that sparked off an unprecedented wave of pilgrimage throughout Europe. The foundation by noblemen of monasteries, churches and hospices, including those along the pilgrims' routes, 'for the salvation of their souls' can be linked to this phenomenon.

The popularity of the pilgrimage to Santiago increased even further with the composition in the early twelfth century of the *Liber Sancti Jacobi*, a work written specifically with the intention of glorifying the saint. Amongst other items it contains a guide to the pilgrims' routes and a list of the saint's miracles. An implied authorship of the text by Pope Calixtus II (1139-45) and an address it contains to the abbot of Cluny give a strong indication of the parties involved in its composition. Furthermore, the text extols not only the merits of the holy places in Santiago itself but also, significantly, those of the churches along the pilgrims' routes, and notably those in France.

By the twelfth century, then, the routes to Santiago had become firmly established. Four major roads traversed France, often along already established Roman roads or trade paths, separately crossing the Pyrenees in order to come together at Puenta la Reina near Pamplona. From here a single route continued on to Santiago for a further 600 km. The southern and middle approach routes on the French sides of the Pyrenees, which passed through Le Puy, Limoges and Toulouse, were frequented by pilgrims from Burgundy, Italy, Hungary, Austria and southern Germany. It was, however, the northern one, which took in visits to the grave of St Martin at Tours that was most popular with French, Flemish and northern German pilgrims. Moreover, it is at the port

2. The Mullingar excavation. (*Westmeath Examiner*)

of Bordeaux, long established as a trading point with Britain and Ireland, that many Irish pilgrims are thought to have joined the other groups.

The concept of pilgrimage was well known in Ireland. Already during the early Middle Ages *peregrinatio* was an ideal followed by many, in particular by clerics. Yet, in most cases, it differed from what we now consider to be a typical pilgrimage and what was also the medieval continental equivalent: a journey to a holy site with the intention of returning. In what Kathleen Hughes called 'perpetual pilgrimage', the Irish pilgrims typically betook themselves to remote areas in and around Ireland, Britain and the continent. They were driven either by religious motives, by the urge to expiate their sins or by mere wanderlust, but they rarely returned. Instead, they were instrumental in founding religious houses abroad or otherwise gaining employment in a monastery along the way. Equally, when the historical record speaks of the commencement of a *peregrinatio* to a monastery within Ireland, more often than not the reference is to a journey undertaken at life's end in the knowledge that there will be no return. In fact, the records of most of those that participated in the Irish *peregrinatio* survive only in the archives of the continental monasteries they chose as their new homes. The Irish annals rarely mention expatriates. By leaving the country, pilgrims seemingly ceased to exist for those keeping Irish records.

References to organised voyages to visit famous shrines with the intention of returning home are rare in Ireland. This applies equally to journeys of pilgrims within the country. Regrettably, therefore, we possess few travel reports or itineraries similar to those that survive from other countries. Yet the upsurge in the practice of pilgrimage during the eleventh century seems also to have had its effect in Ireland. The annals testify to the journeys of both nobles and clerics to Rome, often, however, only to record their deaths abroad. This may indicate that some of them travelled towards the end of their lives, with no great hope of return.

Bearing in mind that official visits by the Irish clergy to the papal court could be combined with pilgrimage, it is not surprising that journeys to Rome received most coverage. The other two important destinations, Jerusalem and Santiago, being more arduous and demanding, were understandably accessible to fewer pilgrims. Rare as references to Jerusalem may be, we have the good fortune of possessing the itinerary of an Irish pilgrim, the Franciscan brother Symon Semeonis, who left Ireland together with his companion Hugh le Luminour, another Irishman of Anglo-Norman descent, in 1322. His observant and detailed account provides us with a wealth of information.

The pilgrimage to Santiago receives hardly any mention in Irish documents before the fifteenth century so we have to rely on continental sources for information. The Irish Benedictine monasteries in southern Germany, the *Schottenkloster,* whose beginnings can be traced back to the late eleventh century, are a very strong reminder of the impact of the Irish *peregrinatio* abroad. Hundreds, if not thousands, of Irishmen (and some women) left their country to become members of these communities. Thus, it does not come as a surprise that the mother house at Regensburg, and some of its most important dependencies, were dedicated to St James who had by now become the universal patron of pilgrimage. We know that at least one of the monasteries, St James at Würzburg, possessed a relic of its patron, which is said to have been presented by the local bishop at the consecration in 1139. It was in the *scriptorium* of the mother house that a history of Irish *peregrinatio* was written in the thirteenth century. Here we are told that 30,000 saints, some of them old and debilitated, left Ireland with the permission and benediction of St Patrick, one group setting off for the Holy Land, the other for Rome. A third group left to visit the graves of the apostles, including that of *beatissimus Jacobus* in Compostela. It was of course in the author's interest to promote pilgrimage, having come to Germany as a *peregrinus* himself, but we can also detect from this work that, by the thirteenth century, pilgrimage from Ireland to all of these places must have become quite popular.

Evidence from Ireland itself tends to confirm this. Foundations of pilgrims' hostels in ports such as Dublin in 1216 and Drogheda where St James' Street and St James' Gate still evoke the original dedication, testify to an increased Irish participation. These hostels, catering for pilgrims who might have travelled long distances overland already, most probably also existed in other harbour towns, such as in those of the south and west, accustomed to trade relations with France and Spain.

It is indeed plausible that pilgrims would have used established trade routes, and that the ships that brought goods to and from Ireland also provided berths for pilgrims. This would almost certainly have been the case for pilgrims taking the boat to Bordeaux or to other ports of the Saintonge before joining others on the *via turonense*, the overland route to Spain. Unfortunately, however, documentary references are mostly only to taxable goods contained within cargoes and not to passengers. By the fifteenth century, however, references to Irish pilgrims begin to feature more often in documents. At this stage, the direct route by boat to the port of La Coruna, north of Santiago, was preferred by many. Indeed, the 'maritime pilgrimage' now undertaken by Irish and British pilgrims brought about a significant increase in numbers. Although the journey through the Bay of Biscay was certainly nothing to look forward to, once in La Coruna, Santiago could be reached by a comparatively short walk. Ships left Ireland for Spain from Drogheda, Dublin, Wexford, New Ross, Waterford, Youghal, Cork, Kinsale, Dingle, Limerick and Galway, while other Irish pilgrims are thought to have joined their fellows in British ports, particularly Bristol and Plymouth.

Despite the fact that this form of pilgrimage must have been easier than the overland journey, we have many accounts of difficulties encountered by the

3. The Mullingar excavation - note the scallop shell. (*Westmeath Topic*)

travellers. Four hundred Irish pilgrims, returning from Santiago in 1473 on board the vessel *La Mary London,* for example, were attacked and captured by pirates before eventually being allowed to land in Youghal. Similarly, during the fifteenth century, the annals report the loss at sea of many Irish pilgrims, some of them chieftains. Others died soon after their return. These spectacular events naturally impressed themselves on chroniclers, whereas references to the many voyages completed successfully would have been of less interest. Between the middle and the end of the fifteenth century, many hundreds or thousands of Irish people, with only the more powerful among them mentioned in documents, must have embarked on pilgrimage. An interesting example is provided by the two pilgrimages of James Rice, Lord Mayor of Waterford, in 1473 and 1483. He had to apply for leave from his office, and testimony to his great devotion to St James is still visible in a side-chapel of Waterford Cathedral, which he built in honour of the saint.

After the initial upsurge of the twelfth and thirteenth centuries, recurrent plagues and warfare during the fourteenth century had greatly hindered travel. By the fifteenth century, however, both the local economy and native Irish fortunes had taken a turn for the better. The resurgence of the Gaelic families brought new confidence, and saw them join their Anglo-Norman compatriots in the foundation of monasteries and in the reinvigoration of religious life. This new prosperity, together with the improvement of ships and navigation,

4. The Irish Benedictine monastery at Regensburg, Southern Germany, was dedicated to St James. (Schnell and Steiner)

made for expanded trade and also incidentally benefited pilgrimages abroad. The fifteenth century can thus be described as a veritable century of pilgrimage. This was, however, to be once more hindered by the Reformation which heralded a substantial decline in the practice over the next few centuries.

The late twentieth and early twenty-first centuries witnessed an unprecedented revival of pilgrimages in general and of the pilgrimage to Santiago in particular. The 'way to Santiago' has been adopted as a theme by the European Union, signalling the unifying character of pilgrimage from all over Europe. Every year, thousands of people retrace the steps of their medieval forefathers, many of them on foot, horse or even by bicycle. When the Puerta Santa, the door of the cathedral, closed on 31 December 1993, it was reckoned that some three million pilgrims had visited Santiago during that Holy Year. At the same time, research on all aspects of pilgrimage has blossomed, with the publications of Peter Harbison on pilgrimage in Ireland and of Roger Stalley on Santiago leading the way here. Many issues still await to be addressed, however, such as whether medieval Irish architecture shows signs of having been influenced by what the pilgrims saw abroad. The still not satisfactorily explained source of the Hiberno-Romanesque style, or at least of certain of its motifs, may well have had something to do with the style of churches encountered by pilgrims abroad. On the other hand, Stalley has quite rightly pointed out that in the heyday of Irish pilgrimage during the fifteenth century, Irish pilgrims were travelling by ship: 'while the sea routes helped to sustain the popularity of Santiago, they did little to broaden the mind of the many thousands who set sail from the northern ports each spring and summer'. Yet the extent of the impact of pilgrimage during the twelfth and thirteenth centuries is slowly coming to light. Excavations such as those at Mullingar and Tuam add to our knowledge, as does research into the religious institutions of the newly founded towns. The role of the Anglo-Norman monasteries outside the gates of the city walls as hospices for pilgrims is now under review, as is the close connection of the orders of the Templars and Hospitallers with the pilgrimage to Jerusalem.

Following the example of the continent, the revival of pilgrimage routes within Ireland have also generating interest. It is important that Ireland, with her long tradition of *peregrinatio*, should be involved in this new-found interest in one of the great unifying experiences of medieval and modern lives.

The author would like to thank Fionnbarr Moore, Michael Gibbons, Jim Higgins, Ray Linehan, John Mulvihill and Eilis Ryan for their help.

Chapter 2

Festive Irishmen: an 'Irish' procession in Stuttgart, 1617

Hiram Morgan

Major Henry McClintock's *Old Irish Dress* (1943) has been an inspiration and a pleasure to many readers. In this and later editions he assembled many of the sources—written, pictorial and archaeological—relating to Irish costume from the earliest times. In McClintock's enlarged 1949 edition, he drew attention to an Irish procession at Stuttgart in 1617 which appeared in a German book by Georg Rudolf Weckherlin about festivities surrounding the christening of Prince Johann Friedrich of Württemburg and the wedding of his uncle Ludwig Friedrich to Elisabeth Magdalena of Hessen. 'Among these festivities' writes McClintock, 'was a procession, organised by a body of Irish men, perhaps soldiers serving in the Württemberg army, of which there are five pictures together with a detailed description in Weckherlin's book. This procession was in no sense a military display; weapons and armour hardly figure in it. It was rather a pageant intended to represent the faith and nationality of the men who took part in it'. In 1950 John Hennig complemented McClintock's efforts with a short article in which he translated the text relating to the Irish pageant, provided information on Georg Weckherlin and noted earlier German representations of Irishmen, as well as Irish involvement in other court entertainments.

It is highly unlikely that the figures in the Stuttgart procession are real Irishmen. More than likely they are Württemburg court officials or local actors dressed up. Their costumes are far richer and more colourful than other descriptions of Irish dress. The harpers in the procession have little false faces attached to their knees and bums—a sure sign that the participants are masquers. Furthermore, far from passively depicting Irish faith and nationality, this representation of the Irish is part of a larger set-piece exercise in German Protestant propaganda on the eve of the Thirty Years War (1618-48). One can confidently make this reinterpretation because, since the days of McClintock and Hennig, the study of costume books upon which they drew and of court festivities such as Stuttgart has been revolutionised. Sir Roy Strong's *Art and Power: Renaissance Festivals, 1450-1650* (1984) comes most readily to mind.

5. and 6. Taken from Georg Weckherlin's *Kurtze Beschrelbung* (Tübingen, 1618). (Bodleian Library, Oxford)

Costume books, first manuscript and later printed, are major sources for McClintock's depiction of sixteenth-century Irishmen and women. A good case can be made for all these images being purely representational—at best mannequins, at worst total caricatures—rather than drawings of real people from Ireland. Interest in different costumes first became vogueish with the circulation of French and Italian engravings and woodcuts. When Albrecht Dürer did an ink and watercolour drawing of Irish soldiers in 1521, it was one of a series of drawings of people in national dress possibly intended for later publication along similar lines. Significantly his caption runs 'Thus go the soldiers in Ireland', not 'These are Irish soldiers'. About 1530 Christoph

Weiditz put together a full manuscript costume-book after travelling in the Iberian peninsula. His *Trachtenbuch* has coloured drawings of Moors, Basques, and many others whom he had encountered there with an appendix of other nationalities for comparative purposes. One of the latter was captioned 'Thus go the women in Ireland'. Much of Weiditz's material re-appeared a generation later in the first printed costume-books—*Recueil de la diversité des habits* (Paris, 1562) and *Omnium fere gentium nostrae aetatis habitus* (Venice, 1563). Soon other compendiums of costume appeared, mostly emanating from the printing presses of the Low Countries and Germany. These, together with atlases, were the coffee-table books of their day.

Another set of remarkable images which McClintock drew to our attention were the watercolours by Dutch artist, Lucas de Heere, in the early 1570s. He incorporated images of Irish soldiers and of the wild Irish and civil Irish into a large manuscript costume-book in his native Ghent, as well as into a gazetteer of the British Isles for refugees fleeing from the war in the Low Countries. De Heere's drawings were merely adaptations of earlier images. McClintock correctly identified a highly stylised English drawing of Irish soldiers dating from the reign of Henry VIII as the common source of De Heere's and other contemporary images of the Irish. Ironically these observations did not lead McClintock to question the utility of these pictorial sources for costume history, let alone his contention that the dress of these soldiers represented the regional costume of south Leinster where most of them were recruited. Such sources do seem to reflect, or refract, the involvement of Irish troops in Henry VIII's continental wars. What is developed is first a caricature of the bellicose Irish dressed and armed in an outlandish fashion distinct from the European norm. This is succeeded and supplemented by a division of the Irish into wild and civil categories. The third development was the identification of the Irish with Catholicism. The first such image occurs on the frontispiece of John Bale's *Vocacyon to the Bishopric of Ossorie* published during his continental exile at Wesel in 1553, portraying a meek English Christian menaced by a brutish Irish Papist. All three characteristics—the alleged Irish penchant for violence, incivility and popery—come together in John Derrick's *Image of Ireland* (1581) with its famous woodcuts. Derrick *had been* in Ireland, and so his work provided a far more accurate depiction of Irish dress, but there was still a continental link because many of the woodcut experts employed by his London printer were Dutch.

Irish figures also entered the scenarios of Renaissance festivals. These increasingly elaborate events to celebrate royal rites of passage or mark state occasions saw huge expenditures by kings and princes. Despite the entertainment-oriented production values, their underlying purpose, if not the actual content, was always political. The festivals developed out of medieval tournaments, royal entries to cities and disguised or costumed playlets called 'masques'. The tournament element was now less violent, more staged and often had a narrative theme. Huge floats with exotic and antique tableaux passed by interspersed with short theatrical performances. The whole show mixed neo-platonic ideas of harmony with chivalric ideals as a focus for aristocratic unity. The most famous festivals, commemorated in the Valois tapestries, took place under the direction of Catherine de'Medici at the French court. One of her events at Bayonne in 1565 featured a mock battle between British and Irish knights. The British led by the king representing heroic virtue (King Arthur) triumphed over the Irish led by the dauphin representing Love (Tristan and Isolde). Such events gradually became private performances in specially constructed locations and not unsurprisingly, the derived aspects of modern culture—orchestral music, ballet and opera—are still considered elite entertainments.

There were Irish characters in court masques performed for Henry VIII— Hennig opined that the images recast by Lucas de Heere in 1572 may have been masqueraders rather than soldiers. In 1552 William Baldwin staged 'An Irish play of the state of Ireland' for Edward VI. Queen Mary's court witnessed a masque of 'Almaynes, Pilgrymes and Irishmen' in 1557. Her successor, Elizabeth, watched another masque entitled 'The Irish Knight' at Whitehall on Shrove Tuesday, 1577. Also staged in Elizabeth's honour were the Accession Day tilts on 17 November each year. In the 1584 tournament 'some of the servants were disguised like savages, or like Irishmen, with their hair hanging to the girdle like women, others had horses equipped like elephants, some carriages were drawn by men, others appeared to move by themselves, altogether the carriages had a very odd appearances'. This citation shows development towards the full-scale festival and also possible Irish representation. The same is evident in the 1594 portrayal of Captain Thomas Lee as an Irish kerne by the Flemish artist Marcus Gheeraedts. Sir Henry Lee, Elizabeth's champion and organiser of her tournaments, was the uncle and patron of this English captain soldiering in Ireland. His dress, far more ornate and revealing than that of an ordinary kerne, would have been more suitable for the annual tilts than an Irish battlefield. Furthermore, it is widely recognised to have been derived from 'Hybernus Miles' by the Dutch engraver Abrabam de Bruyn for a German costume-book in 1578. In this instance and others, the costume-books were either used to kit out individuals attending and acting in the court festivals or plagiarised to stylise the various participants in the subsequent commemorative publications.

The annual tilts gradually died out under the Stuarts but the court masque reached its apogée under Ben Jonson and Inigo Jones. We have the text of Ben Jonson's *Irish Masque* performed on 29 December 1613 against the backdrop of an Irish Catholic delegation to England following a chaotic opening session to the parliament in Dublin. This has the familiar Irish dichotomy. King James is interrupted by Irish servants—Dennisse, Dermock, Donnell and Patrick—

7. Irish woman from Christoph Weiditz's *Tratenbuch* c.1530. (German National Museum, Nuremburg)

speaking with a brogue, uttering superstitious Catholic oaths and dancing jigs to the sound of the bagpipes. They are displaced by their masters, Irish ambassadors to court, who reveal themselves by casting off their mantles. These men bring in a bard who proclaims to the more harmonious sound of the harp that James, the king foretold in Irish legend, will be a bringer of unity and civility to Ireland. Georg Weckherlin, the impresario and recorder of the Stuttgart festivities, came to Britain on diplomatic visits between 1609 and 1615. He may have attended court events such as this and more than likely the celebrations surrounding the marriage of Elizabeth Stuart to Friedrich Elector Palatinate earlier the same year. He may even have ventured further west if the beginning to an ode to drinking 'I was also in Ireland once' is more than mere poetic licence.

In 1615 Weckherlin returned to his native Württemburg, a small frontline Protestant principality in Southern Germany facing the militant revival of Catholicism in nearby Bavaria and Austria. The following year he organised a festival for the christening of the duke's son, Friedrich. This was a pretext for another gathering of the members of the Protestant Union along the lines of Duke Johann Friedrich's own wedding in November 1609 which had seen an eight-day festival attended by thirty-nine princes and princesses, fifty-two counts and countesses, over six hundred nobles and ladies backed up by nearly two thousand servants. At Weckherlin's event Elizabeth Stuart and her husband the Elector were the guests of honour. Consequently he published an English version of the proceedings dedicated to the princess entitled *Triumphall shews set forth lately at Stütgart* (Stuttgart, 1616). The evening after the christening, present-giving and feasting, the noble guests assembled in a large hall of the palace. The show began with the entry of four huge heads each containing six masquers representing respectively western, northern, eastern and southern nations. The first head disgorged the westerners—an Englishman played a lute, and an English gentlemen danced a galliard; then a wild Scotsman dancing to the sound of a Scottish drum and finally an Irishman who danced for a compatriot playing a harp. The fact that the English dancer was dressed in 'white silver cloth, as English lords were wonted to use some twenty years ago' suggests the influence of costume-books. Out of the other heads sprang Frenchmen, Germans, Laplanders, Spaniards, Italians, Poles, Africans, Turks and Native Americans.

Next day the action moved to the tilt-garden of the palace where Duke Johann Friedrich playing King Priam of Troy arrived attended by the three Graces, the nine Muses and other characters and warriors from the Trojan War. Next Friedrich the Elector Palatinate appeared as the Roman Scipio fresh from his victory over the Carthaginians in Africa. His victory is reported as justice driving out injustice. Then a nymph representing Germany saluted the princes and discord represented by four men tied back to back was ceremonially defeated by concord. Tilt matches and various other shows followed, interspersed

8. Battle between British and Irish knights, Bayonne festival, 1565. The participants here are distinguished by devices on their shields rather than national costumes. Centre detail of 'Tournament' tapestry from Frances Yates, Valois Tapestries (1959).

with political comment. The four sons of Aymon (aristocratic opponents of the Emperor Charlemagne in a medieval romance) carried banners protesting *Pro Religione, Pro Libertate, Pro Patria* and *Pro Amicis* and held shields decrying neutralism and infighting. Venus and Cupid were captured and then rescued. Ludwig Friedrich, the duke's brother, fought for the honour of three English ladies styled Derby, Pembroke and Winchester. A king from far-off Madagascar turned up to challenge the European knights. The climax was a series of foot-battles between aristocrat-led teams of Germans, French, knights of Malta and Amazons. On the following day there was a carnivalesque anti-masque with chimney-sweeps staging mock tournaments. There were other days set aside for rest and conversation, hunting and fencing and the week's celebrations ended with fireworks and a cannonade on Sunday night.

Weckherlin was appointed secretary, interpreter and court historiographer to the Duke as a result of the successful organisation and publicity of the 1616 event. He organised further festivities for the christening of the Duke's second son and the marriage of his brother Ludwig in 1617, and produced a commemorative programme entitled *Kurtze Beschreibung dess zu Stutgarten bey den Furstlichen Kindtauf und Hochzeit jungstgehalten Frewden-Fests* (Tübingen, 1618). These followed a similar format but were even more political as tension escalated towards the outbreak of the Thirty Years War in Bohemia. In the 1617 festival there was a distinct Irish section in a pageant of representing ancient and modern nations. The Irish segment was preceded by the Spanish parade. Four court officials were dressed up as nasty and vainglorious Spanish knights—'El espantoso Espadesternudo', 'El fuerte Ferraguto', 'El orrible Rodomonte' and 'El terrible Mandricardo'. Of these nasty and vainglorious Spanish knights, the last two, drawn from Ariosto's epic romance *Orlando Furioso*, had fought for the Moors against the Christians.

While the crowd was still laughing at the send-up of the Spaniards, they were 'attracted by the ringing of many brightly sounding bells and by pitiful crying and fearful clamouring. After being cheered by so many divine heroes and nymphs, they beheld a group, very strange and curious, but of stately attire, moving into the lists in the following order'. German heralds on horseback ushered in three Irishmen on foot. The middle one carried a yellow banner with the symbol of a hand testing gold on a touchstone and an inscription *Sic spectanda fides* which Weckherlin translates as 'Thus faith and belief would be freely exhibited'. His two sidekicks rang 'bells to call the people to devotion'. Then came another three Irish impersonators 'apparently worn out by many a long pilgrimage and vigil' carrying outsize rosaries, the middle one dressed in purple holding a large key with a shamrock handle.

9. The masque of twelve nations, opening scene of the 1616 Stuttgart festival, from Esaias van Hulsen, *Repraesentatio der Furstlichen Aufzug und Ritterspil* (Stuttgart, 1616). (Folger Shakespeare Library)

Next were three harpers dressed in yellow, blue and green respectively 'playing together in sweet accord, according to their national custom'. Then two elaborately-dressed footmen and their splendidly-arrayed master mounted on a snow-white steed 'bedecked with a red cover and bridled in the Irish fashion'. A cleric and his servant came by sprinkling holy water 'to free the spectators from pain and torment of what followed him'. A huge float representing St Patrick's Purgatory with St Patrick sitting on top hove into view. (Fig.7) 'All kinds of vermin crawling upon it, smoke rising from it, fire and screaming indicate the large number of souls pitifully tormented inside.' Next a female figure 'to warn the mortals and to save them from all fear of the torment represented by the previous scene' carried a cross with an inscription *Solum crede* translated by Weckherlin as 'belief alone helps with suffering'. Then followed two footmen in stripped costume armed with axes clearing the way for their masters on horse-back. Four grooms in feathered caps leading horses brought up the rear.

In a leaflet passed round the noble spectators the three Irish horsemen presented a challenge or defiance. They styled themselves three brothers— Con Crochbragan, Teg Kilmannug and Ned Clochmoga—'insuperable Irish knights of St Patrick's Purgatory'. Having travelled the world cleansing it of vice and vermin, they had been attracted to the noble gathering in Stuttgart as a means of enhancing their knightly reputation. The brothers announced that their 'heroic fortitude cannot be resisted by any knightly adversary, not even the devil himself, because those who behold us as enemies, even the devil himself and St Patrick's whole purgatory (which we have produced here in triumph) are terrified and frightened at our strong hearts and irresistible blows. Therefore, we kindly admonish and earnestly warn them to join devoutly our procession, promising them that we shall protect them, in their knightly honours, not only from all temptations of the devil and hell, but also from all enemies, whom we may encounter'.

Literary sources as well as Weckherlin's own imagination went into the creation of this Irish pageant. In his text he states that he used William Camden's *Britannia* (1586) which had an Irish component for information about St Patrick's Purgatory in County Donegal referring to it as 'the rocky cave of *Ellanu frugatory*' [*recte* Oileán an phurgadóra] about fifteen miles from Lough Erne. St Patrick *mise en scène* with snakes and other reptile- like creatures would have been recognised by the audience. The fact that the Purgatory is more of a hill than a cave may suggest some confusion in Weckherlin's mind with Croagh Patrick which was also known to continental Europeans. For the Irish knights he simply took three short Christian names and tagged them onto Irish place-names out of contemporary atlases. This apparent unfamiliarity with 'Mac' and 'O' surnames seems to cast doubt on his claim to have visited Ireland. Weckherlin proclaims that the horses are bridled in Irish style but here, as in a few other places, the text and pictures disagree because the associated drawings show them to be fitted with standard European harnesses. Presumably the German riders would have fallen off if they had tried to use snaffle bits and ride without stirrups like real Irish horsemen. The weaponry, close-fitting clothes and conical hats of these stage Irishmen do have a passing resemblance to what is depicted in Derrick's *Image*. Though as McClintock himself stated, the rich fabrics that went into their outfits were never used in Ireland.

The message contained in Weckherlin's representation of the Irish would have been obvious to the aristocratic members of the German Protestant Union assembled in Stuttgart. It represented the brand of Christianity which Luther had swept away in Germany. The Irish Catholics which it portrayed are full of superstitions, given to farcical devotions and took piety to extremes. They are slavishly devoted to the cult of saints here represented by St Patrick and torment themselves with pilgrimages such as that to Lough Derg. The emblem on their banner indicates that they were always willing to put their religion to the test. The shamrock key suggests not only that the Trinity is the key to heaven but also that the Irish are aligned with Rome. The clergyman in the parade is clearly identified as Catholic by his biretta, though ironically he could never have gone about similarly dressed in Protestant-controlled Ireland. St Patrick, though referred to by Weckherlin as the apostle of Ireland, does not carry a cross. Rather he has a mitre and crozier and is therefore a Protestant hate-figure—the Catholic bishop. His miraculous casting out of snakes and reptiles would have seemed ridiculous to this Protestant audience. The Donegal pilgrimage site represented here—historically not associated with St Patrick at all in spite of its name—was supposed to give visitors lowered into a dark pit an uncomfortable glimpse of the torments awaiting sinners in purgatory. The selling of indulgences to get time off purgatory had of course been what triggered Luther to launch the Reformation. The culture of indulgences derived from the doctrine of good works. The slogan on the Irish banner *Sic spectanda fides* betrays their commitment to this ostentatious approach to getting redemption; indeed the motto on the cross they are carrying *Solum Crede* is the exact opposite to the famous catch-phrase of the whole Protestant Reformation: *Sola Fide*.

The Irish horsemen, by their challenge, show themselves to be the self-appointed crusaders who will bring back Catholicism with all its fervent display. In this light the fact that superstitious and threatening Irish should follow the anti-Christian Spaniards into the arena is no accident. The Spaniards had already been engaged in a number of military actions on the western borders of Germany in the years leading up to the Thirty Years War and were seen as possible backers for an Austrian Habsburg attempt to overthrow German Protestantism. The outlandish Catholic Irish—who in recent years entered the

10. 'Thus go the soldiers in Ireland' by Albrecht Dürer, 1521. (Staatliche Museen Preussischer, Berlin-Dahlem)

military service of the Spanish Habsburgs in such numbers that separate Irish units had been established in Flanders—were regarded as their most willing accomplices.

Weckherlin's German pageant was a biting parody of the Irish in comparison with the burlesque optimism of Jonson's masque in London four years before or medieval romanticism evident at the Bayonne tournament fifty years previously. Plainly the Renaissance caricature of the Irish was not simply an English phenomenon. The striking thing about the evolution of this representation was the involvement of so many continental Protestants from Dürer onwards. They tended to employ earlier images and ideas rather than work from real life. As a result we have a series of images which accreted characteristics over time. This evolving stage Irishman was a product of European religious reformation as much as English attempts to conquer Ireland. Continental Protestants were attracted by the outlandishness of the Irish; they were also repelled by what appeared to be the absolute antithesis of their beliefs. Through costume-books and pageants the Irish attained a place in the Renaissance world—a world in which all nations were subject to varying degrees of generalisation, misrepresentation and caricature.

Chapter 3

Not only seminaries: the political role of the Irish colleges in seventeenth-century Spain

Oscar Recio Morales

From the end of the sixteenth century, Irish colleges were established in Spain as instruments of a religious and cultural offensive in Ireland on behalf of the Spanish monarchy and the Irish community in exile. Traditionally the religious function of these institutions has been the most stressed—as training grounds for a clergy to go into hostile Protestant-controlled territory. However the Irish colleges, besides being theological institutions, were political instruments of the Spanish monarchy as well as 'think-tanks' forging new concepts of 'Irishness' under the ideological guidance of the Irish communities. It is in this context where new research lines may be opened as a result of the cross analysis of the papers deposited in the main Continental archives (Simancas, Brussels and the Vatican) and the main collection on the Irish colleges held in the Russell Library, Maynooth University.

Between the defeat of the pope's mercenaries at Smerwick (1580) and the arrival of the papal nuncio Rinuccini in 1645, it was the Spanish monarchy rather than Rome which assumed the role of political and religious protector of Irish Catholics. Besides, since the Spanish intervention at Kinsale (1602) the Spanish monarchy was under obligation to the Irish. The Irish hierarchy could not have been clearer when they informed Philip III in 1619 that 'God our lord graced your majesty as the Catholic protector, the champion and the safeguard of his holy church on earth. So it is evident that, in conscience, this forces [the Spanish king] to give a helping hand to the Irish Catholics, as they are oppressed merely because of their faith and the service of your majesty'. The patronage of the colleges was the moral response of the Spanish monarchy to the *razón de religion* (cause of religion), as the Irish insisted. The confessionalisation of the inhabitants of Ireland under the rules laid down by the Council of Trent was necessary. However, along with this religious function, the political role and the propaganda dimension of the colleges is very evident. In 1623, after his embassy in London, the count of Gondomar asserted that the Irish colleges constituted an essential part of the Spanish policy on the British Isles, 'because [the colleges] have been artillery which, for God's service and your majesty's, caused a battery of mighty result in those kingdoms, so it is

11. Philip III – in 1619 the Irish hierarchy pointed out that as 'Champion and the Safeguard of His Holy Church on earth' he was duty-bound to help Irish Catholics. (Museo del Prado, Madrid)

(and it will be) an annoyance to the king of England, a source of fear to him and of authority to your majesty'. This 'authority' stressed by Gondomar was the matter of prestige or *reputación*—using the exact contemporary term—of a monarchy which, besides the conservation of her dynastic patrimony, kept as one of her ideological and basic principles the defence and conservation of Catholic religion. This defence became Madrid's permanent political aim in Ireland. In fact, Spanish political thought in the second half of the sixteenth century and first half of the seventeenth finds its roots in a deep respect for religion and its importance for policy. Thus, religion was an indispensable and constitutive component in the social and political establishment of the *Monarquía hispánica*.

The Irish colleges, as main pillars of this defence, were also used in order to strengthen Madrid's political authority over the Irish. The colleges educated and formed not only priests, but also lay Catholics. In this way, the Irish colleges had a complementarity between the religious sphere and its political use compatible with Spanish policy itself. In 1610 the rector of Salamanca came to the Castilian parliament and requested economic help to maintain and construct a house for the sons of the Irish Catholics, 'always true servants to the Spanish Crown that, apart from the service thereby done to the Lord, this assistance will oblige the entire Irish nation to serve at any time the Spanish monarchy'. Nearly 3,000 ducats were granted to the construction of the house. Another 310 ducats were disposed in order to put up, next to the altar where a mass was be said each year, the royal coat of arms and a legend recording what assistance was given and why.

Finally, the education of Irish priests in Spanish territories allowed the monarchy to exercise a direct influence on the Irish ecclesiastical hierarchy. As was usual in Spain itself, the crown had a decisive influence over a large range of provisions to episcopal sees in Ireland. As early as 1570 Philip II nominated an Irish graduate of Salamanca, Malachy O'Moloney, as Bishop of Killaloe. In 1597 some Irish bishops requested and achieved from the king the nomination of a Spanish Franciscan, Fray Mateo de Oviedo, as Archbishop of Dublin. Fray Florence Conry, also a Franciscan in permanent connection with the court, reached the archdiocese of Tuam in 1609; Hugh McCawell and Thomas Walsh, both ordained in Rome by the Spanish Cardinal, Gabriel Trejo, obtained the archdioceses of Armagh and Emly respectively in 1626.

So, Madrid used the Irish colleges as instruments of its particular defence of the religious orthodoxy applied elsewhere in Europe and to the Irish case in particular. The monarchy used the Irish colleges in an attempt to preserve its political influence in Ireland. Furthermore it used the same facilities to strengthen a patron-client relationship with the Irish groups in exile. This patronage was possible because the colleges themselves played an essential role in the creation of a political ideology amongst the émigré group.

The impulse for the establishment of the Irish colleges also came from the exiled Irish themselves. The seminaries were a means of strengthening Irish political ideology, though the Irish in them did not necessarily constitute a united front. In order to elicit a positive response from the Spanish monarchy, the Irish community developed an ideology based on their hypothetical Iberian origin, their unbreakable links to Rome and the services rendered to Spain. The success of this ideology allowed a great number of Irishmen to enter the Spanish social, political and administrative structures, a process that exploited the Irish colleges in the territories under Spanish rule.

They brushed up ancient chronicles and revised texts in order to offer a new 'Spain-friendly' image of Ireland. This effort was part of a more general task of creating a new history of Ireland which was characteristic of the first half of the seventeenth century. This trend eventually led to the compilation in Flanders of the famous *Annals of the Four Masters* or to important individual works such as Seathrún Céitinn's *Foras feasa ar Éirinn*.

The descriptions of Ireland and its inhabitants were often idealised. The Irish attempted to erase, or at least to weaken, a negative image promoted by English chroniclers of an isolated island occupied by 'savages'. Irish colleges accepted and spread abroad a myth which eventually became an irrefutable historical fact: the Spanish roots of the Irish. The end of a speech made in Salamanca in 1618 made this absolutely clear: 'All the historians (as far as I know) agree, and with them some Spanish as well, (and nobody denies it) that the Irish are descended from the Spanish, coming from that part which is called Iberia (from which, Hibernia seems to come). Their chief is called by our people Miles, brave prince of Spain'. It is no wonder that the Irish began to exploit the Milesian myth to demand economic assistance. A memorial which the Irish college directed to Philip III in 1610 stated that 'we have been living in this Kingdom, in the city of Salamanca, for twenty years without having the possibility to own a house of our own, always living in rented houses with discomforts and hardships, spending the money set aside for our food on rent. It would be a pious and merciful deed if your highness took charge of giving us a house, since, as your highness knows, our forefathers gave his, being both generous, not just one, but many houses; not just a corner, but a whole kingdom'.

The case of Salamanca is not an isolated example: the memoir of the Irish College at Santiago began by noting that 'Ireland is now conquered by the heretics and suffers the heretical drought of Catholic faith and religion. The sons of Ireland are coming to the same land from which their forefathers left, demanding support. Thus, they hope for help and welcome from it'. While supporting and promoting the political ideology of the Irish in exile, the colleges helped to develop and strengthen in Spain the image of Irish religious perseverance. Thus, the memoirs and reports produced by the colleges constantly refer to a 'golden age' of Celtic Christianity and to the Irish contribution to the foundation and growth of the religious orders on the continent. Though the Irish proved their perseverance, holding out against Henry VIII's reforms, the Irish émigré community asserted that the preservation and the strengthening of the Catholic faith would in the final

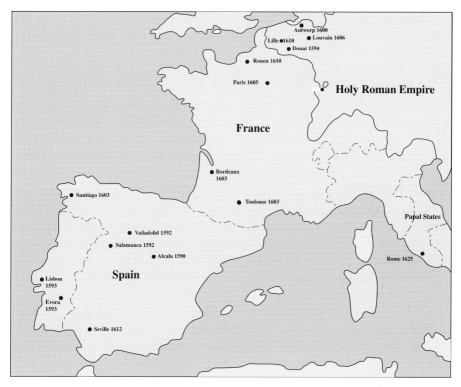

12. Irish Colleges in Europe.

analysis be due mainly to the efforts of continental seminaries—and it was the
Spanish monarchy's business to protect them.

  These general interests of the Irish community were threatened by particular
interests and differences from within. The colleges were the chosen arena
for a bitter struggle between the Franciscans—generally associated with the
Old Irish, Gaelic natives—and the Jesuits—associated with the Old English,
descendants of the Anglo-Normans who settled in Ireland from the twelfth
century onwards. With the progressive spread of Jesuit influence over the
colleges, the Irish Franciscans feared for their special position with the Spanish
monarchy. The control of these institutions was fundamental as they were a
certain and undoubted source of patronage and, as a consequence, of political
control over the different Irish communities in the Spanish territories.

  The work of the Society of Jesus in Ireland dated back to 1542, only two
years after the founding bull of the order, promulgated by Pope Paul III on
27 September 1540. Although its early missions to Ireland were far from being
a conspicuous success, there is no doubt that the reforming movement begun
by Ignatius de Loyola saw the Irish colleges as a great opportunity. Since its
foundation, the order considered education as the most effective and successful

weapon to fight against religious ignorance. Consequently, a network of college-seminaries was set up all over Europe, starting from the establishment of a college in Messina in 1548, of the Roman College in 1551 and of the German College in 1552.

The Jesuits' designs on the Irish colleges in Spain immediately collided with the Irish community of Gaelic origin, who were mostly from Ulster or Connacht by birth and traditionally connected to the Franciscan order. Franciscan monks had deeply influenced Gaelic-Irish chieftains and their decisions since their first establishment in Ireland in 1433. Thus, from the end of the sixteenth century, they became the major defenders of the Irish question before the Spanish court. Around 1590, the Franciscan Bonaventure Naughten, Bishop of Ross, reported in Madrid about the qualities and merits of his countrymen. The Spanish friar Mateo de Oviedo, and Bishop of Dublin since 1597, belonged to the Franciscan province of Santiago. The most significant case is that of Florence Conry, who had arrived as confessor to Hugh O'Donnell in 1602. After the latter's death, he held the most important position in the Spanish court, as far as the Irish question was concerned, until his death in 1629. He held the post of councillor—*protector de los Irlandeses*—a newly established official post. Conry worked out lists of his fellow countrymen and confirmed the living conditions and situation of each of them. Besides, he communicated all the information directly to the Spanish court.

During the first years of the seventeenth century, it was Conry who led the hard-nosed Franciscan reaction against the newly-won Irish Jesuit influence within the court. Salamanca became the main battlefield. Conry accused the Jesuit superiors of the college of being partial and unfair in the admission of students, and unfit to manage the institution. In practice, the Franciscan friar warmly supported two students from Ulster who had not been admitted to Salamanca. Unlike the relatively anglicised provinces of Leinster and Munster, the provinces of Ulster and Connacht remained predominantly Gaelic. Furthermore, Ulster was the home of the most ancient Irish lineages, like O'Neill and O'Donnell, who claimed direct descent from the ancient kings of northern Spain. The myth claiming Spanish roots for the most important Irish aristocratic families was also exploited to mark out differences between the two Irish groups. Irish Jesuits were often from the Old English merchant class from the cities of the Irish eastern and southern coast—traditionally Anglo-Irish areas, Catholic but loyal to the English Crown. On the other hand, the Gaelic-Irish expressed a contempt for trade and stressed their complete military commitment to the Spanish authorities. This attitude appealed to strict Spanish social principles of purity of blood and the renunciation of those occupations such as trade which were not deemed 'noble'. These were still very important *desiderata* at the beginning of seventeenth century for obtaining a military post.

13. Franciscan Florence Conry, who arrived in Spain in 1602 as confessor to
     Hugh O'Donnell, was *protector de los Irlandeses*, the most important Irish
     position at the Spanish court. (St Isidore's College, Rome)

14. Donal Cam O'Sullivan Beare – a leading figure among the Irish exiles in
    Spain. (St Patrick's College, Maynooth)

The Society of Jesus' refutation of Conry's accusations gives a clear picture of the deep disagreement and division within the Irish in exile, the consequent loss of prestige before Spanish councillors and the Spanish monarchy's inability to put an end to the controversy. Just when everything seemed to hint at a reduction of the dispute, the polemic and the tension moved on to Santiago de Compostela, Galicia, home to an important community of Gaelic-Irish Kinsale exiles, in particular families led by the O'Sullivan Beare and the O'Driscoll. Under their protection, a college was set up in Santiago. At first it was intended for the education of those youths sent to Spain by the Irish nobility as proof of their loyalty to the Spanish king. As a consequence, its graduates were not destined for the clerical mission in Ireland. The conflict broke out in 1611 when Philip III commanded that the college should be put under the Society's administration but it took two further years before Jesuits could enter the college.

If in the case of Salamanca it was Conry who led and supported the Old Irish cause, this time it was an aristocrat living in Galicia and of Gaelic-Irish roots who took up the cudgels. Donal Cam O'Sullivan Beare, knight of Santiago since 1617, was a leading figure amongst the Irish exiles in Spain. Using his position the Count of Berehaven renewed the initial secular character of the college. Thus, Santiago would be the basis of an educational system to form the Irish nobility's sons, who, under the protection of the Spanish monarchy, would demonstrate complete loyalty to the Catholic church and to Spain. As in the case of the Royal College of Alcaláde Henares, the Irish aristocrats would be educated in order eventually to enter the monarchy's bureaucratic and military machinery. Besides, O'Sullivan suggested that the Irish students admitted to the college should be accepted by order of the governor of Galicia, upon positive report by 'the most prestigious and powerful members of this nation (the Irish nation) who are to be found in Spain'. In effect Irish noble families would control access to the college.

The dispute between the Old Irish and Old English carried on after Salamanca and Santiago. In 1624, the council of state examined a report sent by the 'Irish prelates and lords' complaining about the Jesuits' intention of obtaining total administrative control of the Irish colleges in Portugal (then ruled by Spain). It denounced the fact that 'colleges admit students who are totally ignorant of the Irish language' and argued that preference be given to 'those who have served the Catholic religion and your majesty'.

As before, each accusation put forward by the Gaelic Irish against the spread of the Society's influence repeated similar arguments: the hypothetical Iberian roots of the Gaelic-Irish; their blood purity and loftiness; their dedication to soldiering more than to any other occupation; their use of the Irish language; and their constant loyalty to the Spanish crown. The colleges were the scene of a struggle bound to strengthen the Gaelic Irish's traditional privileged position with the monarchy. Nevertheless, the Spanish authorities preferred to avoid favouritism and tried, in vain, to foster a single Irish party. The Spanish monarchy failed to understand the complex Irish socio-political and religious framework. This was probably the chief obstacle to Spain's overall strategy in Ireland.

Madrid adopted a cultural solution which combined the fulfilment of its perceived obligations towards the faith under threat in Ireland and the pursuit of its pragmatic political goals there. The chosen instrument was patronage of the Irish colleges and the support of their intellectual production— catechetical, devotional and historical works. This network of colleges and seminaries was sheltered by Castilian universities which embraced as an integral part of their educational programme the defence of the Catholic religion and its spread and growth.

The seminaries and scholars in the universities of Spain (and Spanish Flanders) allowed the Irish to develop their political ideology and to produce a history which contested the supposed English legal rights over the conquest of Ireland. Nevertheless, control over the colleges caused a fierce dispute between the Irish, which clearly highlighted the deep disagreements between the two Irish Catholic groups, the native Gaelic and those of Anglo-Irish roots. In the seventeenth century the *Catholica Hibernorum natio* was still far from establishing itself as an Irish political nation. The Irish abroad attempted to preserve the interpersonal networks on which the majority of Irish society based itself. The Irish lords were seeking better social recognition within the court, which generally turned into a rise in salary (*entretenimiento*). For instance, the O'Driscolls 'certified' members of their family and worked together with the O'Sullivans, both being families from the south-west of Ireland. If a clergyman was in close contact with an Irish lord in Ireland, he usually tried to preserve and strengthen that relationship when he went abroad. In short, the sympathy between different families and different regions was more important than any concept of an 'Irish nation'. This was the context of the political offensive of the Old Irish in their attempt to restrict Jesuit control of the Irish colleges in Spain.

Chapter 4

From Baltimore to Barbary:
the 1631 sack of Baltimore

Theresa Denise Murray

In the early hours of the morning of 20 June 1631, a ship's boat, with a crew of captain, ten sailors and guide, its oars wrapped in oakum to dull the sound, rowed ashore at Baltimore, County Cork. The purpose of this clandestine journey was to scout the layout and defensive strength of the small coastal community. The sack of Baltimore, the only recorded instance of a slaving raid by corsairs in Ireland, was part of a wider pattern across Europe, encompassing not only the entire Mediterranean region but also the Atlantic seaboard as far north as Iceland. Slave-raiding of Christians by Muslim corsairs became common from the late fifteenth century onwards, coinciding with the expulsion of the Moors from Spain. In his comprehensive study *Christian slaves, Muslim masters* (2003), Robert Davis saw a direct correlation between the two. He proposed that by expelling the Moors from Spain in the final years of the fifteenth century, Ferdinand and Isabella created an implacable enemy, as well as fostering a new dynamism among Islamic North African communities, which manifested itself as a passionate and conscious desire to settle accounts with Christendom.

Slave-raiding as an economic and ideological weapon was not confined to the Muslims of the Ottoman Empire and North Africa. European seafaring powers engaged equally in the taking of Islamic ships and the use of their crews as slave labour. In addition, the European trade in African slaves was also beginning to increase in volume and efficiency. Indeed, the Atlantic slave trade peaked as the Barbary trade went into decline in the eighteenth century. Nonetheless, the Barbary slave trade in the sixteenth and seventeenth centuries for a time outstripped European transatlantic slave-trafficking.

In the sixteenth and seventeenth centuries the Ottoman Empire appeared to be in the ascendant, while the Spanish empire, crippled by state debt, was struggling with continual warfare on a variety of fronts. In England domestic tensions between king and parliament were coming to a head. France had been riven asunder by the wars of religion, and the Netherlands was locked into a costly war of independence with Spain.

1600

ABDVLGVAHID,

LEGATVS REGIS BARBARIÆ
IN ANGLIAM,

ÆTATIS:42.

15. Abd el-Ouahed ben Messaoud ben Mohammed Anoun, Moorish
ambassador to Queen Elizabeth I, 1600. The political will on the part of
the authorities to redeem slaves was compromised by such diplomatic ties.
From 1628, King Charles I was deep in negotiations with commissioners
from Salé, Morocco, which resulted in a mutual trade pact. (University of
Birmingham)

The sack of Baltimore, with its mixture of opportunism, careful planning and clockwork execution, was typical of the techniques employed in corsair land raids. On 17 June 1631, two vessels sailing out of Algiers—a 300-ton Dutch-built man-of-war, armed with twenty-four pieces of ordnance and crewed by 200 men, and another vessel of approximately half the size and ordnance—captured a ship from Dartmouth 'betwixt England and Ireland'. Corsairs used a variety of duplicitous methods to effect the smooth capture of a target ship, including running up the flags of friendly nations, wearing European clothing and hailing crews in their native languages. Aboard their prize was Edward Fawlett and a crew of nine. Having stripped the ship of any useful goods, the attackers scuttled it.

By 19 June the raiders were off the Old Head of Kinsale, where they captured two fishing-boats from Dungarvan, one captained by John Hackett, the other by Thomas Carew, both containing five-man crews. The two twelve-ton boats, now manned by corsairs, joined the little flotilla, which continued westward. Aboard the lead vessel Captain Morat Rais, a Dutch convert to Islam with extensive experience in the North Sea, demanded that Hackett pilot them into Kinsale. Perhaps aware of the presence of the *Fifth Lion's Whelp,* under the command of Captain Hooke of the Royal Navy, in the harbour, Hackett allegedly persuaded Rais to continue on to Baltimore.

Baltimore was a familiar harbour to many seamen and had a chequered and controversial history. In 1605 Thomas Crooke purchased a 21-year lease on the town from Sir Fineen O'Driscoll, and set about enticing English settlers to the area. According to a 1608 report from a Spanish ship, most of the native Irish elected not to remain. Crooke is believed to have chosen Baltimore with the specific intention of using it as a supply point for pirates, a charge he was called to answer before the Privy Council in 1608. Although he was eventually acquitted, the verdict may have been influenced more by a political desire to see an English presence in West Cork than by any genuine belief in Crooke's innocence. When one considers a contemporary Venetian assertion that Baltimore was one of the two chief nests of English pirates, the charges of piracy against the town gain a measure of credence. By 1631 Baltimore was a small English enclave surrounded by the hostile O'Driscolls. The town relied on the sea and was struggling financially following the death of the energetic and charismatic Crooke.

The raiding party was first sighted off Castlehaven. Owing to the Dutch construction of the ships, as well as the possibility that the flags hoisted were those of a friendly nation, observers did not recognise the imminent danger. About 10 o'clock on the night of 19 June the ships anchored east of the mouth of Baltimore harbour. A small boat containing Morat Rais, Edward Fawlett and ten crewmen rowed the not inconsiderable distance to the Cove, a small shingle beach approximately 2km from the main settlement. Fawlett, acting as guide, demonstrated great familiarity with the town and coastline, guiding them to shore and providing a comprehensive outline of the layout and the whereabouts of any men likely to provide resistance. Having familiarised themselves with the town, the reconnaissance party returned to their ships to plan the attack.

At 2am on the morning of 20 June, some 230 men, armed with muskets, landed at the Cove. Quickly and silently spreading out, they divided up and waited at the doors of the twenty-six cottages along the shoreline. At a given signal, brandishing iron bars to break the doors and firebrands to torch the buildings, they launched a simultaneous attack on the sleeping inhabitants. The terror of the population can only be imagined as they were wrested from their beds by strange men speaking an unknown language. Ironically, Joseph Whitehead, an earlier captive, described his captors' style of dress as one that did 'much resemble that of the ancient Irish'.

In the initial foray 100 people were seized. Thomas Corlew and John Davis were killed in the fray. Morat Rais then deployed 60 armed men in an ambush formation along the track leading to the town; taking between 120 and 140 men with him, he continued along to the main settlement, intending to mount another surprise raid.

John Hackett, singled out in subsequent correspondence as an 'Irish papist', accompanied Rais on the raid. Hackett's motivation was not explored in his testimony and must remain a matter of speculation. Repeating their tactic of a simultaneous surprise attack, the marauders entered forty houses, rifled thirty-seven of them and captured more victims before the alarm was raised by William Harris, who awakened his neighbours by firing a musket. As another of the inhabitants began to sound a drum to rouse the population, Rais realised that the element of surprise had been lost and retreated back along the track to the cover of the ambush site, and thence to the Cove. The corsairs lost no time in returning to their anchored ships with their booty of twenty men, thirty-three women and fifty-four children and youths, to add to the crews of the Dartmouth ship and the Dungarvan fishing-boats. Captain Hooke later claimed that an additional '30 men at least from Kinsale' were taken, but no mention of these captives appears in subsequent documents. Indeed, if men were taken from Kinsale, Hooke's delay in responding, given this forewarning of pirate activity, seems very irresponsible.

From the narratives of ransomed captives, it is possible to piece together the probable events that took place aboard ship. Many recounted an initial period of harsh treatment for the men in order to 'break them'. For the first hour or so any male captive who did not keep out of his captors' way was severely beaten, and in some instances actually hacked to death in a bloody frenzy. Owing to their high retail value, women and children were treated with relative kindness; curtains were erected to allow privacy, facilities for washing were offered, and they were allowed complete freedom of movement below decks. Icelandic

16. A slave market in Zabid, Yemen, 1237. The actual sale price achieved depended on the abilities of the individual, plus an estimation of how high a ransom could be demanded for them. (Topkapi Saray Museum)

narratives recounting a 1627 raid led by Morat Rais emphasise the kindness shown towards children by his crew.

Prior to sailing, five captives were returned to shore—two elderly people from Baltimore along with Hackett, Carew and Fawlett. Hackett was later tried and condemned to death at a sitting of Cork Assizes; there appear to be no records of Fawlett and Carew's fate. Between 3pm and 4pm, the two ships hoisted anchor and, with a total of 154 captives, began the long voyage back to Algiers and the slave auction. On 10 August James Frizell, the English consul, reported the arrival of eighty-nine women and children and twenty men from Baltimore, two more than were claimed in the State Papers to have been taken.

Inhabitants of the town who had managed to escape in the confusion had immediately raised the alarm. On 21 June Sir William Hull wrote to the earl of Cork, expressing his concern at two good pilots having been taken from Baltimore and his willingness to send 'two sakers and shot to Baltimore and Crookhaven, but there is a complete lack of powder'. Frantic efforts were made

17. 'Remember the Poor Prisoners' – an Englishman collecting alms for the
redemption of slaves, from Marcellus Laroon's *The cryes of the City of
London* (London, 1688). (Folger Shakespeare Institute)

by local people to effect a rescue. James Salmon of Castlehaven unsuccessfully tried to persuade a Mr Pawlett, who had a ship lying at anchor, to pursue the raiders. He also wrote to Captain Hooke, urging him to set sail with all speed. Hooke replied that he was unable to comply owing to a lack of provisions and ten months' arrears of pay. He bluntly stated: 'We cannot go to meet the Turks . . . until we are victualled'. It was several days before Hooke arrived on the scene, by which time the ships were long gone.

Hooke later reported a rumour that the Algerians had been captured off the coast of Spain. A vitriolic correspondence of blame and counter-blame soon erupted. The earl of Cork demanded that Captain Hooke be removed from his position, while Hooke sought to transfer blame to a Bandon supplier whom he claimed was negligent and corrupt, resulting in a lack of provisions.

The Baltimore captives were helpless victims awaiting their fate. In Algiers, Frizell reported that all had arrived alive and requested funds to pay for their release. These funds were not forthcoming, owing to the English government's newly adopted policy of not paying ransoms, as it was believed that to do so would encourage the taking of hostages and act as a disincentive to sailors to defend their ships.

Detainees were immediately taken to the *basha*, an official who had a right to ten per cent of all booty, including slaves. The rest of the captives, with men and women segregated, would have been sent to slave pens. There they were paraded, chained and nearly naked, while prospective buyers inspected the merchandise. Those not sold in the initial auction were housed in storage facilities or *bagnios*—large, unsanitary blocks that supplied casual, and expendable, labour on a contract basis. Children had usually been removed from their families by this point and a process of acculturation had begun. There were exceptions, however. Among the 232 captives ransomed by Edmond Cason in 1646 were three children, all male, who were redeemed along with their mothers. Of the total number repatriated by Cason, the majority were men, with only eighteen women, whose average price far exceeded that of the men: Elizabeth Alwin of London cost 356 and a quarter dollars, while Mary Bruster of Youghal fetched 300 dollars, the average price for a man being 150 dollars. The ransom prices were determined by the original cost price, though Cason did suspect that the figures had been inflated.

The actual sale price achieved depended on the abilities of the individual, plus an estimation of how high a ransom could be demanded for them. Hands were inspected to see whether they were calloused, and captives were tortured to reveal the identity of any wealthy individuals. Those who had skills such as carpentry or military experience were highly valued, while others were condemned to a short brutal life as a galley slave or labourer on one of the *basha*'s many building projects. White women were highly valued, and most would have been bought as items of prestige, destined to spend their lives as concubines; for many of them this would have been a life of comparative luxury, any drudgery being assigned to black slaves. There are few references to women being raped, although there is a report of a young woman being despoiled while still ashore during the Icelandic raid of 1627. Whether the lack of records is due to such attacks being considered unremarkable and thus going unrecorded or because they did not occur is a matter for conjecture.

The children, usually raised as Muslims and by all accounts treated with the utmost gentleness, would eventually form the bulk of a highly efficient slave corps within the Ottoman army; others were purchased and raised in the homes of local people, seemingly becoming members of the family. Young men, aged from thirteen to seventeen, were subject to considerable cruelty at first, often being castrated and/or forced to convert to Islam before being dispatched to the furthest points of the empire.

Of all the Baltimore captives there are few of whom it can be stated with any certainty that they were eventually ransomed. Edmund Cason reported paying the sum of 150 dollars for the release of Joan Broadbroke, either the wife or daughter of Stephen Broadbroke, and a paltry 86 dollars for Ellen Hawkins. Ellen's name does not appear on the original list of captives. There are, however, five unnamed women simply listed as 'maid', and it is probable that Ellen was one of these. The two women, having spent fifteen years in captivity, returned safely to England. Their eventual fate is as yet unknown, as is the fate of the other 105 people, and merits further investigation.

18. A view of Algiers from Pierre de Montmartin's *Neuwe Archonologia Cosmica* (Frankfurt, 1646). (Library of Congress)

The political will on the part of the authorities to seek out and protect captives was questionable when one considers that from 1628, King Charles I was deep in negotiations with commissioners from Salé in Morocco, the other main port of white slavery, that resulted in a mutual trade pact being signed with Mulay al-Walid, emissary of the sultan, between November 1631 and February 1632. In 1633 Frizell reported that only seventy captives were available for redemption, 'the rest being dead or turned Turk'. He did report the ransoming of an unnamed woman by 'a Mr Job', but gave no further details. In addition to the two Baltimore captives, Cason secured the emancipation of ten of the 120 captives taken from the packet ship *John Filmer* off Youghal in 1641.

By the late eighteenth century the balance had shifted, and the North Atlantic sea powers, in particular England, owing to growing naval pre-eminence, were beginning to occupy the dominant position. The widely held belief that the Ottoman Empire was in decline gave impetus to European colonial attempts to form outposts in North Africa and to challenge the Ottomans militarily. The expanding power of the Royal Navy allowed it to successfully combat Islamic slave-raiding, an activity which, ironically, had been kept viable by a British policy of exchanging arms for captives.

Initially, Baltimore seems to have recovered. By 1632 small units of cavalry were stationed along the coast, beacons were erected on strategic headlands and the town was beginning to rebuild. That same year, however, there were rumours of a planned return by corsairs. In December 1631, Benjamin Whitcomb wrote to his brother from Marseilles, warning of another planned attack by 'Turks'. For many of the inhabitants of Baltimore, the fear was too great and the majority of those who elected to stay in West Cork moved further inland to Skibbereen. In 1790 one visitor to the town described it as being nothing but a decaying fishing village and rotten borough.

For the captives life was never the same again. Those who were ransomed usually ended their lives in destitution, viewed with suspicion and unable to resettle. A small minority profited from their experiences through the sale of lurid captivity narratives. The majority of those who 'turned Turk' blended seamlessly into the fabric of life in North Africa, sometimes rising to positions of influence and prestige that would have been impossible in class-conscious Europe, while others died of culture shock. Of those who remained Christian, most quickly succumbed to overwork and hard usage, their identities and fate unknown. Whatever their fate, all the captives had one thing in common: their lowly status as pawns in a global power game that had been played between Islam and Christianity since the eighth century.

Chapter 5

The Scotch-Irish & the eighteenth-century Irish diaspora

Patrick Fitzgerald

Probably no other ethnic group in North America has had as much ink spilt on the usage of the terminology applied to define them than those labelled the Scotch-Irish or Scots-Irish. Those exploring the historical phenomenon of migration from Ireland to North America now use the term, which always retained a certain ambiguity, less frequently. The Scotch-Irish, however, are firmly lodged in the established mental map of American ethnology and the challenge to replace this terminology remains unfulfilled. The period from the 1980s onwards has seen considerable historical revision in relation to eighteenth-century Ireland and the stream of emigration which emanated from it. The growing awareness of the more heterogeneous make-up of the Irish diaspora and the current debate about Ulster-Scots culture and identity in Northern Ireland perhaps converge to make this an apposite juncture for a review.

As an American construct, the exact nature of the migrant fusion between Scottish and Irish influences has often been prone to a degree of haziness. The profusion of popular historical literature on the far side of the Atlantic has generally served to reduce visibility further. The establishment of a connection between those leaving the northern half of Ireland for colonial America in the early eighteenth century and British settlers in Ireland in the previous century has proved problematic. The term 'Scotch-Irish' clearly implies that those who emigrated across the Atlantic were descended from those who came to Ireland from Scotland and yet we know that the majority of British settlers in seventeenth-century Ireland originated in England and Wales. Even in Ulster, where Presbyterians from the Scottish lowlands settled in greatest numbers, there was substantial settlement by those from England and Wales. That Presbyterians, predominantly of Scottish origin, formed the largest element within Ulster emigration to colonial America is not disputed but Anglicans and Quakers of English stock also left. Kerby Miller has estimated that 30 per cent of those leaving Ulster for colonial America were Protestant but not Presbyterian. Furthermore, the notion of complete ethnic and religious separation and segregation in the century before large-scale emigration commenced around 1716 is untenable.

19. *The Sally* sails from Belfast for Philadelphia, May 1762. (Stephen Conlin)

This point was acknowledged a generation ago. Writing of seventeenth-century Ulster, Estyn Evans noted that 'there was much more intermarriage, with or without the benefit of clergy, than the conventional histories make allowance for. Many planters became Catholics and many natives became Protestants.' In short, the boundaries of a separate Ulster-Scots community were ill-defined a century after the Jacobean plantation.

The majority of those taking ship from ports such as Belfast, Derry or Newry in the early part of the eighteenth century were not, by and large, leaving a country where their families had been resident for over a century. Apart from the fact that there was significant, if spasmodic, return migration to Scotland during the seventeenth century, the greatest volume of Scots came to Ireland during the second half of the century. A contemporary observer reported the influx of 50,000 Scots in the 1690s. Although almost certainly an exaggeration, the combination of low land prices in the wake of the Williamite war and sustained harvest failure leading to famine conditions in Scotland ensured a strong *fin de siècle* surge in westward migration across the North Channel. Evidence suggests that those who came after 1695 and as a response to the severest of famines in Scotland were significantly poorer than previous Scots settlers. Historians of the Scotch-Irish, often with notions of 'doughty Scots planters', have not generally framed their subjects as famine immigrants and this is certainly a depiction absent from much of the late nineteenth and early twentieth-century historiography.

Another feature, which has bedevilled much of what has been written about those described as the Scotch-Irish, is the absence of historical context and little account of change over time. The impression of almost seamless continuity from one generation to another is quite pervasive in the history that was fashioned a century ago and indeed remains potent in many popular histories of our own time. For example, Rory Fitzpatrick's *God's Frontiersmen: The Scots-Irish Epic* (London, 1989) referred to the lawlessness of the English/Scottish border region in the sixteenth century as a factor explaining patterns of behaviour among Ulster Presbyterian settlers in eighteenth-century backcountry America. Yet convicted border reivers were a small minority of those who settled in the northern half of Ireland during the early seventeenth century. Over a century later when the first large-scale emigration from Ulster got under way, the society they left was far removed from a lawless frontier zone. Furthermore, the context of settlement in the New World was not homogeneous and was arguably much more influential in shaping patterns of settler behaviour than distant ancestral experience.

Billy Kennedy's *The Scots-Irish in the Hills of Tennessee* (Londonderry, 1995) alluded to the link between the traditional music carried to the southern backcountry in the eighteenth century and contemporary country and western music. Kennedy made reference to the 'strong Scots-Irish blood' which flows through the veins of Dolly Parton and the 'definite Ulster-Scots roots' of Ricky Skaggs, another top American country music star. Kennedy then presented the narrative from the musical documentary at Dolly Parton's East Tennessee theme park as confirmation of the link. He quoted the following passage: 'And so they came...a strong willed people who forged their homes out of this region and brought their love and beauty with them. The deeds of our Scots-Irish ancestors are blended with the skills of the musicians who seized the smokies' fiery spirit and this heritage has been passed on from generation to generation'. The clear emphasis in both accounts is on the continuity of traits and traditions almost in isolation from geographical context or historical change.

The sparseness of material artefacts relating to the migration and settlement of emigrants from Ulster to North America during the eighteenth century has also played some part in shaping this emphasis on what one might call persistent folkways. The difficulty of demonstrating palpable change over time through the evolution of everyday objects is substantial and has placed a heavier burden on non-material culture in the exploration of Scots-Irish heritage. Given the fact that those who left Ulster for colonial America were not on the whole materially rich, the study of their music, song, lore, leisure pursuits, etc. has a great deal to contribute to an understanding of their experience. It is essential, however, that the methodologies employed in this endeavour are thorough and not ultimately ahistorical.

The Irish eighteenth century is viewed very differently today than was the case a generation or two ago. Book titles serve to chart the course of revision, with 'penal era' and 'hidden Ireland' giving way to 'new foundations' and 'the long peace'. The appreciation of the rapid commercialisation of society, particularly in Ulster, has obvious implications for the interpretation of Ulster emigration to colonial America. In broad terms, religion as an explanatory 'push' factor has given way to economic factors. The exodus of large numbers of Presbyterians from Ulster had more to do with the regime of rents, leases and harvests than it had with persecution by the Anglican church and state. There is also a growing recognition of change over time. The traditional landmark date employed to differentiate early modern from modern emigration was 1776, the commencement of the American Revolution which effectively put America off limits for the following six years. Yet in many ways this date reflects American factors rather than Irish. Even in these terms the picture is changing. The rapid switch from passages undertaken by recourse to indentured servitude, before the Revolution, to those made by fare-paying passengers thereafter, has to be challenged in the light of recent work by Marianne Wokeck. Her comparative study of Irish and German migration to colonial America found that of the northern Irish landed in the ports of the Delaware Valley between October 1771 and May 1772, only 9.7 per cent had been unable to pay their fare in advance.

It is clear that the context that conditioned the emigrant's decision to leave was also changing. In short, the emigrant of 1720 was not subject to the same set of forces as the emigrant of 1770. On the basis of a revised interpretation of Irish and indeed Atlantic history in the eighteenth century, it is evident that detectable and significant changes in the character of emigration were occurring from around the middle part of the eighteenth century. In the first half of the eighteenth century the Irish economy remained structurally weak in relative terms. The vulnerability of society to mortality crises such as those suffered during the late 1720s and during the famine of 1740-41 was perhaps the starkest measure of this economic fragility. The major surges in emigration during this period were closely correlated with subsistence crises. Throughout the seventeenth century food crises had impelled Ireland's poor to migrate internally towards the towns, particularly Dublin and towards Britain and even the near Continent. By the 1720s the New World had become an additional option for those escaping hard times at home. It is notable how little contemporary comment was directed towards the downturn in the linen trade during the later 1720s as a factor in conditioning emigration. The industry, even in its Ulster heartland, was not yet fully developed. Harvest failures triggered those cited by Archbishop Boulter as 'the middle and meaner sort of people' to escape the oppressive regime of rising rents and restrictive leases. Despite the 'Black '47'-like panic to get out of Ireland and the fact that demand for shipping

20. Emigrants from the period after 1763 were generally equipped with greater skills than those who had gone before. (Ulster American Folk Park)

outstripped supply, the bulk of emigrants from Ulster ports were able to pay their fare. More than anything this probably reflected the capacity of tenants to realise capital during a crisis by selling their interest in a holding, what would later become known as the 'Ulster custom'.

The decade and a half before the outbreak of the American Revolutionary War witnessed the strongest and most consistent wave of emigration from the northern province to the ports of the Delaware valley. L.M. Cullen has convincingly argued that this exodus was different in character from the largely crisis-driven emigration of the 1720s and 1740s. Rather, he suggests, that this exodus should be viewed as 'an entirely new development', shaped by wider and positive economic changes. The spectacular expansion in Ireland's Atlantic trade after mid-century was accompanied, particularly in Ulster, by intensive development of the linen industry. The net consequence of this accelerated development was the transition to a pattern of migration which drew upon the more skilled more informed, and provided greater scope for individuals who made rational choices based on perceived opportunities across the Atlantic. It should be stressed that emigration from Ulster and indeed Leinster and Munster was particularly voluminous after the end of the war in America in 1782. The achievement of victory over, and independence from, the British Crown served to cast America in a new light for Irish Catholics. The new Republic's esteem was also boosted among Ulster Presbyterians who took particular pride in the achievements of their kith and kin in the New World. Yet if one views emigration from Ulster between 1760 and 1800, the break

21. This gravestone from Raloo parish, near Larne, County Antrim, illustrates the impact of famine in early eighteenth-century Ulster. (Patrick Fitzgerald)

caused by the Revolutionary War takes on more of the appearance of a hiatus than a transformer. The oft quoted words of John Dunlap, Stabane-born printer of the Declaration of Independence, written in a letter home in 1785, successfully capture the outlook of many Ulster emigrants who had crossed the Atlantic in the decades since the end of the Seven Years' War in 1763. In criticising the Irish parliament's attempts to stem emigration, Dunlap offered the opinion that 'the young men of Ireland who wish to be free and happy should leave it and come here as quick as possible. There is no place in the world where a man meets so rich a reward for good conduct and industry as in America.'

One of the difficulties with the use of the term Scotch-Irish as a description of Ulster Presbyterian or Protestant immigrants to colonial America is the very limited evidence that this was a term which such settlers applied to themselves. Where it was used as a label in the eighteenth century at all, it tended to be applied by Tidewater colonial governors in a pejorative way. Those colonial Americans who had occasion to refer to immigrants from Ulster overwhelmingly opted for the simple designation 'Irish'. Not only did these eighteenth-century Ulster Protestant settlers not refer to themselves as Scotch-Irish, they generally accepted the label 'Irish'. This is certainly not to say that no distinctive identity or sub-culture existed among Ulster Presbyterian settlers of Scots heredity. Anglo-American governors had few doubts about the existence of such a phenomenon. Nonetheless, outright rejection of the designation 'Irish' was the exception. The transition to a pervasive association between Irishness and Catholicism lay in the future with the mass mobilisation of the O'Connell era.

In seeking to explain why the Scotch-Irish are so firmly lodged in the established mental map of American ethnology today, one must look back to the second quarter of the nineteenth century. An increasingly voluminous flow of Irish Catholics to the United States from the 1820s onwards accompanied the increasing exclusivity of an Irish identity as the preserve of Irish Catholics. Although increasing cleavage between Protestant and Catholic Irish-Americans was evident from the 1820s, it was the mass migration of relatively poorer Catholic immigrants during the Famine decade (1845-55) which decisively compounded separation. In an era of increasing nativist reaction, Protestant Americans of Irish origin had fresh incentive to cultivate an ethnic identity that stressed disassociation from an Irish-American Catholic entity. In 1889 the Scotch-Irish Society of America was organised and its annual congresses sought to popularise the expression Scotch-Irish as the appropriate designation for those who traced their lineage back to the Ulster Presbyterian immigrants. The fact that large numbers of those immigrants and their offspring, particularly in the American South, had left the Presbyterian church for other evangelical Protestant denominations such as the Baptists and Methodists served to muddy the waters further. In 1897 the American-Irish Historical Society met for the first time in Boston and over the next decade and a half, the interwoven threads of two centuries of emigration from Ireland to America were consciously unpicked and disentangled. Was it, one wonders, entirely coincidental that at the same time back in Ireland, nationalist and unionist increasingly squared up to each other over the thorny issue of Home Rule?

A pioneering scholarly work on the subject was Robert. J. Dickson's *Ulster Emigration to Colonial America 1718-1775* (1966). Whilst Dickson was well aware of the explicit subjectivity of much of the historiography and fully acknowledged that emigration from Ulster was not homogeneously Presbyterian, his work remained tightly focused upon the emigrant flow from Ulster ports alone. This fact no doubt influenced Audrey Lockhart's *Some Aspects of Emigration from Ireland to the North American colonies between 1660 and 1775* (1976) based on research of emigration from northern *and* southern ports.

Subsequent publications widened the frame within which eighteenth-century emigration from Ulster or Ireland can be considered. James Horn's 'British Diaspora: Emigration from Britain, 1680-1815', in volume II of *The Oxford History of the British Empire* (1998), sets Irish emigration in a British Isles framework. One of the interesting insights provided by Horn is the potential for future comparative analysis of migration patterns from early modern Ireland and Scotland. In much of what has been written about the Scotch-Irish there is surprisingly little reference to those who had come to America directly from Scotland. Marianne Wokeck's *Trade in Strangers: The Beginnings of Mass Migration to North America* (1999) examined Irish immigration to the middle colonies alongside German, the most substantial other ethnic group of immigrants. In relation to the issue of distinctive patterns of emigration from Ulster, her conclusions are interesting. The most important difference between emigrants from Ulster ports and those from ports elsewhere in Ireland was the greater extent to which the former travelled as paying passengers, rather than indentured servants and left as family groups rather than as individuals who were predominantly male. This is clearly an important point and has obvious implications in relation to settlement and integration in colonial America. At the same time, however, direct comparison with contemporary German emigration reveals characteristics that were more similar than different between Irish emigrants from north or south. Set against the German experience, Wokeck concluded that Irish emigrants as a whole had easier access to trade, communications and transportation channels to carry them across the Atlantic. Furthermore, there was interconnection between Irish ports in terms of trade and a proportion of those ships that left Ulster ports called into southern ports, very likely gaining passengers in the process. Dublin's role, in particular, exercised an important link between Ulster and the rest of Ireland. A strong commercial relationship existed between Ulster and the capital city and it may be more than coincidence that the subsistence crisis of the later 1720s, which was most intensely felt in the north, also saw very substantial emigration through Dublin.

It may be hoped that further work of a comparative nature will improve our appreciation of the similarity and difference that characterised migration from different regions within Ireland and between emigration from this island, and other parts of Europe. As research, publication and debate proceed, the challenge of overhauling the terminology of the nineteenth century may, in the twenty-first, be realised.

Afterword

Penned two decades ago, this short article betrays the frustration of an historian engaging with a literature often peculiarly fixated with stressing difference and ignoring commonality with the obvious 'other' in the equation – Irish Catholics. The persistent determination to stress Scotch-Irish or Ulster-Scots traits and traditions in defiance of geographical context or historical change marked out a remarkably durable popular stereotype. In 2012 American historian Warren Hofstra edited a volume which collectively challenged many of these essentialist notions and highlighted the extent to which those who claimed this ethnic identity had always been engaged in a process of negotiation. Whilst celebrating that conclusion one remained very conscious that the focus on Scots-Irish experience therein remained limited to the century and a half before 1830. So if the article's author was to change anything about the 1999 original today, it would be to decouple the ethnic group from the eighteenth-century chronological constraint. From the vantage point of 2019 we can fully appreciate how so many of those who had contributed to the historiography of these migrants and their descendants failed to ask the question – what happened next? Few looked over the precipice of 1800 to find out what happened to subsequent generations of Ulster Presbyterians. To be fair one honourable exception to this statement was Maldwyn Jones. In 1980 Jones acknowledged in his entry on the Scotch-Irish in the *Harvard Encyclopedia of American Ethnic Groups* that 1,075,000 emigrants had left the province of Ulster between 1851 and 1899. He further noted that Ulster emigration was heaviest in this half-century from the most heavily Protestant counties of Antrim and Down. Thus, we can deduce that Ulster Presbyterian emigration was significantly more voluminous in the later nineteenth century than at any point in the eighteenth century. Arguably, however, the strongest sense of being 'written out of the story' related to the absence of Ulster Presbyterians from the traditional narrative of the Great Famine (1845-51). In 2016 Rankin Sherling shone a bright light in this direction and revealed that for Presbyterian clerics, transatlantic migration reached a distinct peak in the late 1840s. That Presbyterian and Catholic demographic decline in Ulster between 1831 and 1861 was broadly similar (18 per cent and 19 per cent) tended to confirm that Famine emigration was, in fact, a central element of Ulster Presbyterian experience. In this sense one might argue that an important future task is to understand better the Scotch-Irish and the nineteenth-century Irish diaspora. We should perhaps recall that it is only within the past generation that we have come to appreciate that the big story of Scottish emigration was much less about the romanticised exodus of the Highland clans than a grittier story of rural-urban migrants to, and of, the Scottish lowlands relocating overseas.

Chapter 6

Revd James MacSparran's *America Dissected* (1753): eighteenth-century emigration and constructions of 'Irishness'

Kerby A. Miller

In the 1700s Irish emigrants to America were remarkably diverse, especially in comparison with the apparent homogeneity of the Famine and post-Famine migrants of the mid to late-nineteenth century. Although a majority were Presbyterians from Ulster, a third or more were Anglicans (members of the established Church of Ireland), Quakers, Methodists, and other Protestant dissenters, as well as Catholics, from all parts of Ireland. Even individual emigrants, such as James MacSparran, could reflect the variety and ambiguity of contemporary 'Irishness'. Yet in his *America Dissected* (1753), the first Irish emigrant's guidebook, MacSparran synthesised a broad if vague concept of 'Irish' identity that may have prefigured the inclusive nationalism of the 1790s.

MacSparran was born in 1693 in County Londonderry's Dungiven parish, over half of whose inhabitants were Irish-speaking Catholics, and was raised by his uncle, Dungiven's Presbyterian minister. However, James MacSparran was not a typical 'Ulster Scot' of lowland Presbyterian ancestry. Traditionally, the MacSparrans were Scottish Catholics and closely allied with the MacDonnells of the Isles, Gaelic-speaking Highlanders (often called 'Irish' by Protestant lowlanders) who in the 1640s were driven out of Scotland to Ulster. James MacSparran's own ancestors apparently avoided expulsion by conforming to Presbyterianism, but in the 1670s or 1680s they migrated to Dungiven from the Mull of Kintyre in Argyll, where Scots Gaelic (then interchangeable with Ulster Irish) was still the dominant language. Almost certainly MacSparran learned Scots Gaelic at home in Dungiven, thus explaining his later boast that he could read, write, and preach in Irish. MacSparran attended Dr Blackhall's academy in Derry city and then the University of Glasgow, where in 1709 he received his MA degree. Subsequently, he studied for the Presbyterian ministry and spent several years as a clergyman in Derry city.

Why MacSparran emigrated is unknown, but there is a suggestion that doctrinal or personal irregularities ruptured his association with Derry's Presbyterian ministers. He landed in Boston in June 1718 and soon became

22. Revd James MacSparran. (Bowdoin College, Maine)

minister of the Congregational church in nearby Bristol, at an annual salary of £100. However, MacSparran aroused the enmity of Revd. Cotton Mather (1663-1728), Boston's most eminent Puritan clergyman. Mather had Irish relations and at first had welcomed Ulster Presbyterian immigrants, but he soon condemned most of their clergy as clannish, contentious, and 'profane'. MacSparran soon faced charges of drunkenness and sexual immorality, as well as accusations that his clerical credentials were fraudulent. In October 1719 he sailed to Ireland to secure their confirmation, promising he would return the following June. However, either because his credentials were indeed suspect, or from anger at his treatment by Derry's and New England's dissenting clergy, MacSparran never returned as a Presbyterian divine. Instead, after securing testimonials from the archbishop of Dublin and other Church of Ireland clergymen, he travelled to England and requested ordination in the Episcopalian faith, in what he called 'the most excellent of all churches'. In 1720 MacSparran was ordained a deacon by the bishop of London and as a priest by the archbishop of Canterbury, and was licensed by the Society for the Propagation of the Gospel in Foreign Parts (SPG) as missionary to the parish of St Paul in the Narragansett country of Rhode Island. In April 1721, 'after a very dangerous tedious and expensive passage', MacSparran arrived in the parish he would serve as rector for thirty-seven years.

MacSparran was one of several Irish-born representatives of an American proselytising crusade that the Church of England had launched in the late 1600s. Between 1680 and 1720 Anglican reformers built over a hundred new churches overseas; by the latter date the SPG (est. 1701) had sent abroad more than sixty missionaries, while its sister organisation, the Society for the Propagation of Christian Knowledge (est. 1699), furnished them with books, tracts, and pamphlets. Ostensibly, the SPG's primary mission was the conversion of slaves and Indians, but critics charged that the church's real goals were to impose its bishops, ecclesiastical courts, and tithes on the colonies, to overthrow the Congregational establishments in Massachusetts and Connecticut, and to subvert the colonists' religious and political liberties.

Rhode Island, unlike New England's other provinces, was neither a Puritan nor a royal colony. Its charter granted religious toleration and civil rights to all but Catholics and Jews, and most of its inhabitants were Quakers, Baptists, and other dissenters who felt threatened by the 'invasion' of a church that proved very attractive to the colony's economic and political elites. Thus, whereas in 1700 the Church of England had scarcely existed in Rhode Island, by 1721 another SPG missionary had transformed Newport's Trinity Church into the province's most fashionable congregation. Likewise, although most of MacSparran's own parishioners were ordinary farmers, his 'elegant', 'commodious', and well-furnished church of St Paul's was dominated by men who were 'exceptionally cultured, well-to-do...and secure in the conviction that to be a Narragansett Planter, with large estates and troops of slaves, was a sufficient patent of aristocracy'.

In outward respects, MacSparran's pastorate was very successful. Although his first year in Rhode Island was marred by fresh charges of intemperance and sexual impropriety, MacSparran quickly married Hannah Gardiner, daughter of his wealthiest parishioner, and won his flock's esteem for his erudition and diligence. Within two years, St Paul's congregation had doubled in size, and he also helped establish Anglican churches at Bristol, New London, and elsewhere in New England. MacSparran's biographer describes him as one of the SPG's ablest missionaries; at least three of his sermons merited publication, and in 1737 Oxford University awarded him a doctorate in sacred theology for his 'talents, learning, good deportment, judgment and gravity'. MacSparran moved comfortably in the colony's highest circles and hosted the celebrated Anglo-Irish bishop and philosopher, George Berkeley (1685-1753), during his 1729 sojourn in America. He was solicitous also for the spiritual welfare of the local Indians and slaves—ten of whom MacSparran owned himself.

Yet MacSparran was never reconciled to remaining in America. He hated the harsh extremes of New England weather; the care of his parish—covering 500 square miles and including three other churches—was extremely arduous for a 'portly' man; and his £70 salary was barely sufficient to maintain a lifestyle befitting his social pretensions. While congenial with his flock, he was also pedantic, pompous, egotistical, and intolerant—characteristics that embroiled him in continual controversies with New England's dissenters, who condemned him as a 'hireling priest' and an Irish 'teague'. MacSparran's vigorous advocacy of an American episcopacy infuriated Congregationalists, and at least one of his sermons incited a bitter pamphlet war. Plagued by nightmares of permanent separation from his Irish friends, from the mid-1740s MacSparran was soliciting influential patronage to gain a position as a clergyman in Ireland. In 1751 news of the death of his only brother exacerbated MacSparran's dissatisfaction and homesickness: 'O [that] I were well settled in my own country', he confided to his diary. This was MacSparran's frame of mind when, a year later, he penned to his former Derry schoolmates three letters which in 1753 were published in Dublin and sold for 6d. as *America Dissected, being a full and true account of all the American colonies*.

America Dissected is considered the first Irish emigrant's guidebook, yet MacSparran wrote it not to encourage or facilitate departures but as 'a caution to unsteady people who may be tempted to leave their native country'. On his title page he promised to expose the 'intemperance of the climates…destructive to human bodies', the 'badness of money; [the] danger from enemies; but, above all, the danger to the souls of the poor people that remove thither, from the multifarious wicked and pestilent heresies that prevail in those parts'.

America Dissected was not entirely subjective, and MacSparran provided much information, fairly accurate, about the population, economy, and government of each of England's mainland colonies and West Indian possessions—detailing especially where large numbers of emigrants from Ireland had settled. Yet his Tory prejudices were obvious, particularly concerning society, religion, and 'manners'. His praise was generally reserved only for royal colonies, like New York and South Carolina, where the Anglican church was legally established, or for the efforts of SPG missionaries, like himself, to combat 'schism and heresy',

23. Within a year of his arrival in Rhode Island, MacSparran married Hannah
    Gardiner (1705-1754), daughter of his wealthiest parishioner. From the
    painting of John Smibert. (Museum of Fine Arts, Boston)

[and] 'immoralities and disorders', in other colonies, such as Pennsylvania and
Rhode Island, where dissenters ruled. In MacSparran's view, royal authority
and Anglicanism were mutually supportive and essential to ensure orderly,
hierarchical social relationships. By contrast, MacSparran claimed, the
influence of Presbyterians, Quakers, and other dissenters inevitably produced
'ignorance', 'levelism', 'confusions', and 'anarchy'.

Yet despite his dislike of dissenters, whether from Ireland or elsewhere, his treatment of all those who had 'winged their way westward out of the Hibernian hive' was sympathetic, notwithstanding that most of the immigrants he described were 'Irish Presbyterians...from the North'. For example, MacSparran praised their 'industry' in Londonderry, New Hampshire, as elsewhere in the colonial backcountry, comparing it favorably with the 'destructive indulgencies' of Southern planters. He also lamented that the 'Irish' were 'less esteemed than they ought to be', although their frontier settlements provided Anglo-Americans with a western 'barrier in time of war' with the French and Indians. As he knew from personal experience, prejudice against all the 'Irish', whatever their religion, was especially strong in New England: 'As the Jews had their Nazareth', MacSparran lamented, 'the New-Englanders have their Ireland', noting with satisfaction, however, that the latter were 'as much despised in the other English plantations, as any teague is by them'. Interestingly, *America Dissected* cast no aspersions on Irish Catholics. MacSparran praised (and exaggerated) their influence in Maryland, and he commented approvingly on Philadelphia's 'public and open mass-house'—the

24. The parish church of St Paul, Narragansett, Rhode Island, where MacSparran served as rector for thirty-seven years after his return to America in April 1721. Built in 1707 and originally located in North Kingstown, RI, in 1800 it was relocated to Wickford, RI, where this photograph was taken in 1907.

only one in the colonies. 'Papists are Christians', he wrote, and 'to be preferred to many Protestant heretics I could name.'

A year after publishing *America Dissected*, MacSparran visited Ireland and England, hoping either to find 'a provision on that shore for the rest of his days' or to be consecrated as the Church of England's first American bishop. However, MacSparran's wife died in London, and he returned to Rhode Island empty-handed, purportedly declaring that 'he would rather dwell in the hearts of his parishioners, than wear all the bishop's gowns in the world'. Two years later, on 1 December 1757, MacSparran, aged 64, died at his house in South Kingstown and was buried under the communion table of St Paul's.

One hundred years later, New England's Episcopalians still memorialised Revd. James MacSparran as the 'Apostle of Narragansett'. His legacy in Ireland, however, and even his motives for publishing his letters there, remain ambiguous. Whether *America Dissected* dissuaded many potential emigrants is improbable, for the very conditions that MacSparran condemned in the colonies—their social fluidity and the weakness of royal and ecclesiastical authority—were more likely to attract than to repel the dissenters who comprised the great majority of contemporary migrants.

On one hand, *America Dissected* must be interpreted in the context of MacSparran's many efforts to solicit Irish patronage—to 'raise me up friends, and restore me to my native land'. Certainly, MacSparran's attempt to discourage emigration was calculated to please Anglo-Irish bishops and Ulster landlords who feared further losses of Protestant parishioners and tenants. Yet MacSparran's strictures on America were no doubt sincere, reflecting his instinctive distaste for the crudity, heterodoxy, and lack of deference that characterised colonial society. Thus, *America Dissected* was designed particularly to discourage emigration by others such as himself: genteel, conservative, and pious but 'unsteady' young Anglicans, who lacked 'connections' sufficient to sustain or improve in the colonies the privileged positions they had enjoyed in Ireland.

More broadly, both the vagaries of MacSparran's career and the tone of *America Dissected* may reflect attempts to resolve issues of 'identity' that were intensely personal as well as inevitably political and inextricably linked to his social aspirations. It is intriguing, for example, that all of MacSparran's writings, private and published, displayed a strong sense of 'Irish' identity that transcended ethno-religious distinctions and included, in his applications of the term 'Irish', Anglicans, Presbyterians, and Catholics alike. In *America Dissected* varieties of 'Irishness' were distinguished, if at all, only by religion, and earlier or subsequently common 'racial' or 'national' designations—such as 'the English in Ireland', 'Ulster Scots', 'Scotch-Irish', 'British', and 'Irish' as synonymous with Catholics only—were strikingly absent. Indeed, because of his varied ancestral and cultural background, MacSparran must have appeared, in the eyes of most Ulster Presbyterians and American dissenters, more suspiciously 'Irish' than conventionally 'Ulster Scottish'. To be sure, in 1716 Ulster's General Synod had designated MacSparran's Dungiven parish as a centre for clerical training in the Irish language, yet Presbyterian missionary efforts were paltry, as most ministers disdained a language they identified with 'popery' and 'barbarism'. Of course, conversions to the established church by affluent or ambitious Ulster Presbyterians were not uncommon in the early 1700s. However, it may be that MacSparran's apostasy was in part a defensive or even a defiant response to suspicions and prejudices to which he, because of his personal background, was unusually vulnerable.

In addition, joining a church commonly associated with high Tory principles may have come naturally to a man whose religious and political origins were so at variance from most Ulster Presbyterians' historical experience and mythology. Whereas the latter gloried in their ancestors' persecutions at Stuart hands and their defence of Derry's walls for William of Orange, MacSparran's kin had fought for Charles I against both Scots Covenanters and Cromwell's Puritans, while he himself was sceptical about the results of the Glorious Revolution. Perhaps even more important, MacSparran's conversion to Ireland's official religion enabled him to submerge and employ his rich but dangerously confusing cultural legacy in ways that were assertively 'Irish' and yet also politically and socially advantageous. For the Church of Ireland, although 'English' in its origin and subordination to Westminster and Canterbury, nonetheless claimed the mantle of St Patrick, and as Ireland's 'national' church it proclaimed—and sporadically pursued—the quixotic goal of obliterating the island's most profound religious and civil distinctions by converting, not only Protestant dissenters, but also the 'native' Catholics—and through the medium of their own language, which MacSparran knew intimately. Ironically, by embracing the Church of Ireland, MacSparran could both be 'Irish' and achieve a social and political status denied by law to Irish dissenters and Catholics alike.

Despite his rather unusual background, MacSparran reflected a general trend: the early eighteenth-century transformation among many of Ireland's wealthy Anglicans from a 'settler' mentality to what some historians have called 'colonial nationalism'—an increasing emotional and political identification with Ireland and Irish interests, coupled with a growing estrangement from the English (British after 1707) government and its legal and economic restrictions on Irish Protestant aspirations. The herald of attitudinal change was William Molyneux's *The case of Ireland...stated* (Dublin, 1698), but after 1714—when the Hanoverian succession entrenched a hostile Whig oligarchy in power at Westminster—Ireland's Protestant gentry and Church of Ireland clergy became more vocal in their 'national' or 'patriotic' objections to British policies and patronage in Ireland. Thus, MacSparran resembled his friend,

25. MacSparran hosted the celebrated Anglo-Irish bishop and philosopher
    George Berkeley (1685–1753) during his 1729 sojourn in America.
    (National Gallery of Ireland)

Bishop Berkeley, and Jonathan Swift (1667–1745), dean of Dublin's St Patrick's
Cathedral, in both his high Tory principles and his bitter resentment against
London's appointments of Englishmen to the most lucrative posts in the Irish
church and civil administrations. MacSparran equally resented British Whigs'

insistence that the Dublin legislature repeal the Penal Laws against the Irish Protestant dissenters whom he—like Swift—now despised.

Thus, *America Dissected* may be viewed in the broad context of political conflict between the Irish and British oligarchies, and perhaps it represents a minor contribution to the Irish pamphlet war occasioned by the 'money dispute' of 1752-53. MacSparran's opposition to a rumoured legislative union between Ireland and Britain clearly expressed his alienation from the British administration and his support for the 'patriot' or 'country' party, which voiced (however cynically) the opinions of most Irish landlords and members of the Irish House of Commons. 'I pray God [such a union] may never take effect', he wrote, or 'farewell Liberty. You are greater slaves already than our Negroes; and an Union…would make you more underlings than you are now…[I]f ever you come into a closer connection with the more eastern island', he warned, 'corruption will increase, peddlers be promoted to power, [and] the clergy and landed interest will sink into disesteem, [for] those that are sent to rule you, like those who sometimes are sent here, imagine fleecing to be a better business than feeding the flock'.

To be sure, MacSparran was angling for Irish patronage. Also, among Irish Protestants, generally, this early growth of Irish 'national' sentiment should not be exaggerated. Although they sought validation of their status by reference to Hiberno–Norman or even Gaelic precedents, the members of Ireland's Anglican ascendancy defined Irish interests in their own, narrow terms, and in the 1780s-90s their interests would make most of them fervent loyalists to Britain in opposition to new, more democratic expressions of Irish nationalism made by Presbyterian and Catholic reformers and radicals. Moreover, even in the mid-eighteenth century, ecumenical interpretations of Irishness could flourish better in the New World than in Ireland, with its deep ethno–religious divisions and large Catholic majority. Hence, it is possible that MacSparran discovered his own Irishness overseas—and that residence in America (particularly in New England), where colonists of English descent often ignorantly or wilfully conflated Irish Protestant and Catholic immigrants, encouraged his adoption of the one 'Irish' identity that enabled him to claim superiority over local dissenters, despite their numerical and political dominance. Yet just as MacSparran's beliefs alienated him from the heterodoxy and liberalism of American society, so also his heightened identification with Ireland accentuated his homesickness for his native land. Thus, less instinctively but perhaps no less sincerely than later Catholic composers of Irish exile ballads, MacSparran expressed in *America Dissected* a cultural or even a 'national' aversion to emigration that contrasted markedly with contemporary Irish dissenters' millennial vision of a new Canaan across the Atlantic.

Chapter 7

The Irish and the Atlantic slave trade

Nini Rodgers

It was the Stuarts who introduced the Irish to the slave trade. Charles II returned to the throne in 1660 at a time when it was becoming clear that sugar plantations were as valuable as gold-mines. The Royal Africa Company (RAC) was established to supply slaves to the British West Indies in order to extend production. Irish names can be found among those working for the RAC. Among the most successful was William Ronan, who worked in West Africa for a decade (1687–97). A Catholic Irishman, he rose to become the chairman of the committee of merchants at Cape Castle in present-day Ghana, his career apparently unhindered by the ascent of William of Orange. In the seventeenth century Europeans saw slaving as respectable and desirable.

26. Slaves cutting sugar cane on a plantation established by the Delaps of Donegal, from *Ten views of the island of Antigua* by William Clarke, 1823. (British Library)

It was conveniently accepted that Africans sold into slavery by their rulers were prisoners of war, who would otherwise have been slaughtered. Thus export to the Americas offered them prolonged life in a Christian society. It was a century later, when public sensitivities began to change, that such attitudes to the slave trade were called into question.

In Europe the connection between the Stuarts and Irish slave-traders was not lost with the throne. The defeated James II was conveyed from Ireland to France by Philip Walsh, a Dublin-born merchant, settled in St Malo, who would die on an African voyage. In 1745 Philip Walsh's son, Antoine, provided Prince Charles Edward Stuart with an armed frigate, on which they sailed together for Scotland in a bid to restore the Jacobite line. Antoine Walsh could afford this political gesture because of the wealth he had made from the slave trade. Nantes (with its close-knit Irish community) had emerged as the kingdom's chief slaving port, a starting-point for the triangular trade—manufactures for Africa (textiles, brandy and firearms), slaves for the French West Indian colonies (Martinique, Guadeloupe and St Domingue), and sugar and tobacco for Europe.

Captains and crew did the voyaging; merchants (ship-owners and outfitters/ *armateurs*) stayed at home, funding and organising. Prolonged loading in Africa was the most hazardous part of the operation. The climate was unhealthy and the slaves, still within sight of the shore, were at their most furiously desperate. Fear of revolt, which could be mitigated for the *armateur* by insurance cover, was rife among captains and crew.

By the early 1730s Antoine Walsh had shifted from slave-ship captain to slave-merchant. He never actually experienced revolt himself but his relatives and employees did. In 1734 *L'Aventurier,* outfitted by Walsh's father-in-law Luc Shiell (O'Shiel), spent almost four months on the African coast, moving from port to port in search of slaves. At Whydah the captain went ashore to trade, leaving Barnaby Shiell, Antoine Walsh's young brother-in-law, in command of a crew largely immobilised by fever and dysentery. The slaves rose, cut the ailing pilot's throat and locked other invalid whites below hatches. At this point Barnaby Shiell, with five armed sailors, fired on the Africans. In the ensuing slaughter two crew and forty slaves were killed. The result in commercial terms was the destruction of one-sixth of the cargo. Undeterred by this setback, Captain J. Shaughnessy determinedly pursued his professional objectives, remaining at Whydah until he was finally able to sail with 480 Africans for St Domingue and Martinique. In the future both Shaughnessy and Barnaby Shiell would act as captains for Antoine Walsh.

After the Jacobite defeat, Walsh turned back to slaving, and immediately one of his ships became the scene of a slave revolt. His ironically named *Prince d'Orange* reached Whydah and took four and a half months assembling 245 Africans. As the ship got ready to sail, six women, one with a child at the breast,

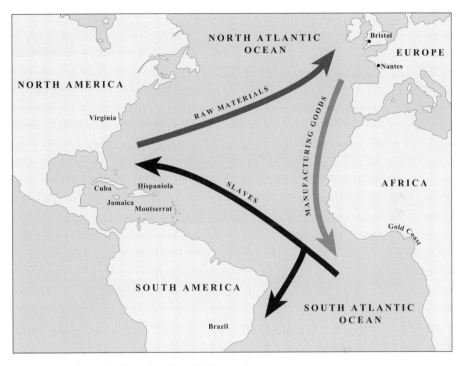

27. The 'triangular' trade. (Sarah Gearty)

threw themselves overboard and drowned. A month later, off the island of San Thome, the remaining slaves rose and killed the captain and two sailors. The crew threatened to resort to firearms but the Africans took no notice and the result was thirty-six dead.

By the eighteenth century Africans were accustomed to guns. The desire to possess them was one of the factors fuelling the trade and bringing about political change as states grew stronger or weaker according to their access to firepower. But those Africans delivered to the ships as slaves were devoid of weapons. In fifty years, the only record of a successful slave revolt on an Irish *Nantais* vessel occurred in 1742, when the 350 slaves on Patrice Archer's *La Sainte Helène* managed to get hold of guns from above deck, set the ship on fire and escape to shore, where the local ruler proved uncooperative in securing their return.

On board Walsh's *Prince d'Orange*, Jean Honoraty (John Hanratty?) replaced the murdered captain and the voyage continued. For an experienced slave-trader it was a familiar professional setback. As far as Walsh was concerned, the real danger to his ambitions had surfaced within Nantes itself. In September 1748 he launched the *Société d'Angole*, the first private joint stock company in France devoted to the slave trade. His aim was to eliminate the weak state monopoly,

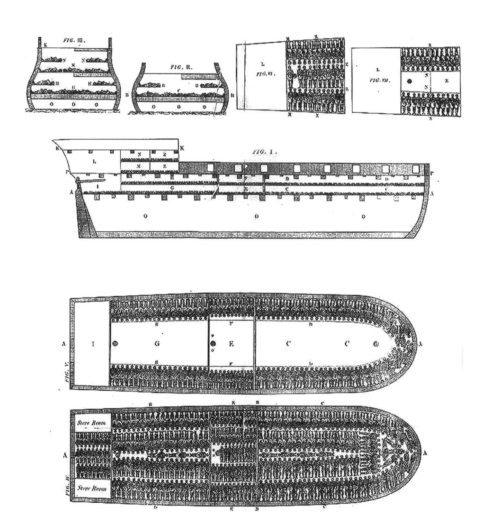

28. *Description of a slave ship*, copper engraving of the Liverpool slaver
Brookes, April 1789, the most famous widely reproduced image representing
slave conditions on the Atlantic crossing ever made. (London Committee
of the Society for the Abolition of the Slave Trade)

Compaigne des Indes (currently drawing most of its income from licensing
independent operators), and to establish the *Société*'s own monopoly of French
trade in Africa. Walsh had risen as an independent himself but now wanted
to prevent the rise of other independents. His financial innovations in France
were to be underpinned by novel arrangements in Africa. The company would
have three large ships stocked with trade goods permanently stationed off the
Angolan coast. Five smaller ships would make an annual Atlantic crossing to
St Domingue, where they would deliver their cargo into a fortified slave-camp.

Almost immediately Walsh's monopolistic ambitions were challenged in Nantes itself by the establishment of a rival joint stock company, the *Société de Guinée*, which proved more successful than its Angolan counterpart. In 1753, when Walsh's company completed the period for which it had been designed, he did not seek to reconstruct it. After launching forty voyages, his career as an *armateur* had come to an end. He left France a few years later to manage the family properties in St Domingue and died there in 1763, slave-trader turned planter/purchaser in a colony which was by then absorbing a shipload of Africans a week. In the eighteenth century Britain emerged as Europe's greatest slave-trader, but the development of St Domingue meant that France became her greatest sugar-producer. This colony, which Walsh helped to build, was envied as the richest gem in the imperial New World, before the opportunity offered by the French Revolution caused it to implode into the Caribbean's first black republic of Haiti.

Antoine Walsh's greatest ambitions had not been achieved in Jacobite politics, nor in establishing the dominance of his company over the French slave trade. Nor had he become France's largest slaver: that position fell to an indigenous French family, the Mauntondons (sixty voyages), who had begun life as shoemakers. Over the years Antoine Walsh had purchased over 12,000 Africans for export across the Atlantic, though not all of them had reached the Americas. No other family from the Irish community in Nantes could claim anything approaching such a score, although two others, the Rirdans and the Roches, emerged as significant *armateurs*. The Rirdan (O'Riordan) brothers, Etienne and Laurent, claiming roots in Derryvoe, County Cork, sent out eleven expeditions during the years 1734–49, purchasing just over 3,000 slaves. Between 1739 and 1755 the Roche family (their roots in Limerick, where they possessed marriage connections with Arthurs and Suttons) organised a similar number.

By the end of the seventeenth century the RAC had lost its monopoly. This opened up the slave trade to individual British merchants, while banning Irish ports from launching direct voyages to Africa. Thus the equivalents of the Rirdans and the Roches (though not Antoine Walsh) can be found in Bristol and Liverpool. Bristol was Britain's premier slaving port from the demise of the RAC until 1740, when Liverpool came to dominate the trade. In this expansive period the Frekes, an offshoot of the County Cork landowning family, could be found among Bristol's leading slave-merchants. Their success over several generations was marked by their move into Queen Square, where they lived in an elegant new building looking out on a handsome statue of William III. Other Irish slave-ship-owners from the same era were Michael Callaghan and John Teague. By the 1760s they had disappeared, to be replaced by John Coghlan and James Connor.

In 1780s Liverpool there were slave-merchants with Irish names: Felix Doran, Christopher Butler, Thomas Ryan, James McGauley and David Tuohy.

But the first four had all been born in that area; only Tuohy had arrived as a young man from Tralee. From the 1750s onwards he and his brother-in-law, Philip Nagle, captained ships to Africa. By 1771 Tuohy was able to write to a Stephen Fagan in Cork that he had 'been in the African trade for many years in which I have made a pretty fortune'. He declared that he was now inclined 'to go no more to Africa but follow the business of a merchant in Liverpool'. Though he gave up sailing to Africa himself after 1771, he continued to despatch ships for slaves. The men mentioned above were professional survivors and successes. In France and Britain many of those emerging as slave-merchants had begun life as captains in the trade. At least five captains died in Africa for every one who achieved the status of merchant.

Probably the most famous (or infamous) slave-ship today is Liverpool's *Brookes*, designed to carry 600 slaves. It began its climb to notoriety in 1789, when the abolitionists produced a diagram of the vessel showing shackled slaves, arranged with mathematical precision, head to toe, layer upon layer, not an inch of space unused. During the American Revolution the *Brookes* was commanded by an Irish captain, Clement Noble of Ardmore. Confronted by an enemy privateer near Barbados, he armed fifty of his cargo and successfully repelled the attack. Commenting that the Negroes fought 'with exceeding spirit', he sailed on to Jamaica, where he sold them on the north coast at Montego Bay.

The number of Scots and Manx captaining Liverpool slave-ships exceeded those from Ireland. But among ordinary sailors the position was reversed and the Irish formed the most numerous non-English group—more than 12 per cent as against the Scots with 9.5 per cent. During the 1750s John Newton, later an Anglican clergyman and author of *Amazing Grace*, captained three voyages from Liverpool to West Africa. Already an evangelical, but still inhabiting a pre-anti-slavery world, he held services on board for the crew, never thinking of extending his religious ministrations to the Africans he was loading and shackling down below. His papers record them as numbers, while his crew names reveal an Irish presence: John Carren, John Megan and James Gallagher. Some of the Irish names presented Newton with greater difficulty. He had trouble in spelling Shaughnessy (Shestnassy) and even more trouble with Cooney (Cooney, Cunneigh and Coney), who took a female slave 'and lay with her brute like in view of the whole quarter deck, for which I put him in irons. I hope this has been the first affair of the kind on board and I am determined to keep them quiet if possible. If anything happens to the woman I will impute it to him, for she was big with child. Her number is 83.'

Many captains and other officers have described the behaviour of common seamen. The crew themselves rarely wrote about their voyages. Two brothers from Ireland have left an account of such experiences, however. Nicholas and Blaney Owen came from an impoverished gentry background. Driven to

29. *View of the deck of the slave ship Albanoz*, pencil and watercolour on paper by Lt Francis Meynell, 1846. (National Maritime Museum, London)

seafaring by their father's spendthrift habits, they spent six years in the slave trade, working first on Liverpool vessels and then deserting to a Rhode Island slaver, where the pay and conditions were better. In 1756 at Banana Island, south of Sierra Leone, their ship was seized by locals, angry because a Dutch captain had recently removed some of their free men. At first the Africans held the crew captive but later allowed them to wander off. The brothers eventually found work with an African-born mulatto who had developed a trading post manned by his wives, children and slaves. For commercial convenience, the Owens built themselves houses at separate points on the Sherbrow River. Nicholas started his journal, recording his past experiences and philosophising on his present isolation in an alien society, describing himself as a 'hermit'.

There was, however, much in Nicholas's lifestyle that was not eremitical; he lived with an African woman and was served by a team of four or five men who helped him to acquire and control the slaves he collected. Generally he referred to this African grouping as 'my people', and on one occasion as 'my family'. In Africa he felt that he had acquired something of the gentry lifestyle he had forfeited at home. But, as he very well understood, it was at the cost of staying there. 'I find it impossible to go of without a dail of dangers and risqué (sic).' When he was well and busy and trade was prosperous, he was not discontented with his situation. But when he was ill it was a different matter. Shuddering with malaria, unable to supervise business, homesickness would strike. 'I have not brought any trade this 2 months, not so much as a *servela* [a term for a little slave]', he wrote. 'I still long more and more for a return to my native country.' Within three months he was dead. Blaney took over the journal to record his brother's passing and his own grief. As the journal survived, Blaney may also have done so. The tale of the Irish brothers, one dying in Africa, the other returning without having made his fortune, encapsulates the experience of most slave-ship crewmen.

Across the Atlantic, in the Caribbean, a group of second-generation Irish emigrants were making fortunes from buying and selling slaves. Since the seventeenth century the Irish had been settling in the Leewards, a string of physically varied and politically diverse islands. Their first choice was St Kitts, until 1713 divided into French and British sectors, and within easy reach of Dutch St Eustatius, a volcanic peak known as the 'golden rock' because of its fame as a smugglers' haven. The authorities, however, increasingly pushed the Irish out of St Kitts onto the tiny volcanic island of Montserrat, where they came to constitute some 69 per cent of the white population, 'almost an Irish colony'. Their presence on nearby Antigua and Nevis was also statistically significant, representing around a quarter of all whites.

Slaves were arriving in huge numbers into the Leewards in the eighteenth century. A Cork man working as an overseer in Antigua in the 1770s, and writing

30. Early twentieth-century 'country huts' on St Kitts, similar to eyewitness accounts of 'thatched and wattled' slave housing on Nevis. (St Christopher Heritage Society)

later to defend the trade, described the arrival of the Guinea ships with slaves dancing, gay, hung with glass beads, as if celebrating a festival. He declared that 'There are one thousand of Irishmen . . . who have been spectators of the merriment'. On Montserrat, Skerrets, Ryans and Tuites busied themselves in inter-island trading, buying slaves from British ships and then re-exporting them, along with cargoes of provisions from Ireland. Nicholas Tuite, son of a Westmeath settler, branched out beyond the Leewards, some four days' sail to the Virgin Islands, where the Danes were developing their colony of St Croix.

While the Danes possessed the capital and mercantile expertise necessary for running such a venture, they did not possess manpower eager or suitable for planting their new possession. It was Nicholas Tuite who solved this problem for them, importing slaves and encouraging other Montserratians, supplemented by individuals from Ireland itself, to move there. Between 1753 and 1773 (the year after Tuite's death), slave numbers are said to have trebled from 7,566 to 22,244, while sugar exports rose from 350 to 8,200 tons. Tuite himself now owned seven plantations there and was part-owner of seven others. In 1760 he journeyed to Copenhagen, where Fredrick V appointed him chamberlain and paid tribute to his role as founder of Denmark's Caribbean empire. Like Antoine Walsh, slave-trading and plantation-owning had made him the friend of kings.

Every group in Ireland produced merchants who benefited from the slave trade and the expanding slave colonies. All slave-trading voyages required minor investors. In the 1750s the Presbyterian McCammons of Newry put money into at least one Liverpool voyage and actually ended up owning a slave. Almost four decades later their cousins James and Lambert Blair, following up West Indian connections, went out to St Eustatius, where they set up as agents, their main source of income derived by purchasing slaves for the Stevenson plantation. At the beginning of the nineteenth century the Napoleonic wars brought Britain the Dutch territory of Demerara. The Blairs, now with funds to invest, were quick to buy land in Demerara and stock it with slaves to develop sugar plantations. In 1833 Westminster emancipated the slaves, paying out £20 million in compensation to the plantation-owners for the loss of their human property. James Blair received £83,530-8-11 for his 1,598 slaves. He thus claimed for more slaves and received more money than any other slave-owner in the British Empire.

Merchants in Ireland's ports and towns were well aware of the importance of the slave trade and the slave colonies. The eighteenth-century economies of Cork, Limerick and Belfast expanded on the back of salted and pickled provisions specially designed to survive high temperatures. These were exported to the West Indies to feed slaves and planters, British, French, Spanish and Dutch. Products grown on slave plantations–sugar in the Caribbean and tobacco from the North American colonies–poured into eighteenth-century Ireland.

31. 'Hibernia attended by her Brave Volunteers, Exhibiting Her Commercial Freedom' – 1780 print by William Hincks. 'Free trade' also meant freedom to enter the slave trade. (National Library of Ireland)

Commercial interests throughout the island, and the parliament in Dublin, were vividly aware of how much wealth and revenue could be made from the imports. The fact that mercantile regulations, laid down in Westminster, meant that 'plantation goods' only reached Ireland via British ports was a source of growing indignation. In 1779 the Dublin parliament and the Volunteers successfully worked together to make Britain's American difficulty Ireland's opportunity, demanding that Westminster repeal mercantile regulations to allow 'a free trade for Ireland'.

The importance of enslaved Africans in furnishing these Irish gains is vividly illustrated in a commemorative print of 1780 entitled 'Hibernia attended by her Brave Volunteers, exhibiting her commercial freedom'. At the centre of the picture a youthful Hibernia, barefoot and barebreasted, hair flowing in the breeze, lifts up both her arms to display a banner bearing the words FREE TRADE. Behind her two armed and uniformed figures stand on guard while merchant ships approach at full sail. In the foreground, flanked by tobacco barrels, are three figures, kneeling before Hibernia to offer gifts. On the left an Irish woman holds out cloths, presumably a reference to the right of Ireland to freely export her textile production. Beside her an American Indian offers an animal pelt. On the right a black slave, strong, sinewy and briefly draped, extends a neoclassical urn, its precious metal representing the untold wealth of Africa and America. These three 'volunteers' carrying riches to Hibernia recall paintings of the Magi and the Christ-child, that biblical scene in which, since the fifteenth century, one of the kings was invariably depicted as an African.

This newly won 'free trade for Ireland' was not restricted to Atlantic voyaging; it also allowed Irish ships to sail direct to West Africa—in other words to enter the slave trade. By 1784 Limerick and Belfast had drawn up and published detailed plans for the launching of slave-trade companies. Both ports contained leading merchant families who had made fortunes in the Caribbean. Creaghs from Limerick can be found slave-trading down the century from Rhode Island, Nantes and St Eustatius, and plantation-owning on Barbados and Jamaica. In Limerick by mid-century John Roche (1688–1760) had emerged as the city's foremost Catholic merchant, richer even than the Creaghs, supplying the West Indies with provisions, buying their sugar and rum, and smuggling and privateering during wartime. A similar pattern was established by Thomas Greg and Waddell Cunningham in Belfast. Their activities in the Caribbean during the Seven Years' War enabled them to improve port facilities at home and to establish sugar plantations in the Ceded Islands.

Such experiences fed patriot ambition to make use of Ireland's new commercial freedom to enter the slave trade. But these plans now proved economically and ideologically backward-looking. By the 1780s more accessible and attractive opportunities were emerging nearer home as Britain industrialised, while simultaneously the rise of an anti-slavery campaign was making a once-respectable trade reprehensible. The projected companies came to nothing.

The slave trade provided labour for the plantation colonies, and these colonies had an enormous impact on Ireland. They encouraged urban growth through the import of sugar and tobacco and the export of provisions. Commercial dairying and beef production changed life in the countryside, generating wealth for some and fostering agrarian unrest among others. By 1780 sugar, though not as inflammatory as tea in Boston, was playing a transforming role in Irish political life. Ireland was very much part of the Black Atlantic world.

Chapter 8

'The entire island is United...': the attempted United Irish rising in Newfoundland, 1800

Aidan O'Hara

In May 1800 Dr. James Louis O'Donel, Catholic Bishop of St John's, Newfoundland, wrote to a fellow government supporter and loyalist, Fr. Joseph Octave Plessis, St John's, Newfoundland, stating that 'I have a vast heap of trouble on my hands as I must be very soon preparing no small number of the Newfoundland Regiment for death. Those villains who formed a plot to take and plunder the town, were strictly bound together with the infamous link of the United Irishmen's oath, and are supposed to have been determined to meet at mass on the 20th of April and proceed thence to the Protestant church and make prisoners of all that were there'. O'Donel had got wind of a plot by United Irishmen in the Royal Newfoundland Regiment of Fencibles to take over the town, if not the entire colony, just a few days before it was to take place, and he immediately informed the authorities. The plan was for the United Irishmen in town to rise with their colleagues in the garrison while the unarmed Protestant officers and soldiers were at church on the morning of Sunday 20 April 1800. The authorities realised that the situation was serious, but they did not panic; the officers kept the suspected leaders of the plot under observation, and when Sunday morning dawned bright and clear, they announced that they would avail of the unusually fine weather to put the entire garrison on parade. Sunday services were cancelled and the soldiers were put through a series of drills and exercises throughout most of the day.

The United Irishmen in the regiment suspected that their officers were aware that something was up, and so they hurriedly revised their plans, fixing the following Thursday for the rising. In the meantime, Bishop O Donel busied himself dissuading the townsfolk from having anything to do with it, pointing out that British military might would inevitably prevail. On the evening of Thursday 24 April, a number of soldiers deserted their posts, with the intention of rendezvousing at a designated location away from the town and the military bases, but they were spotted and all but a few were captured. In spite of the fact that no blood was shed, eight of the United Irishmen were hanged and several more sentenced to penal servitude for life.

32. St John's, Newfoundland, seen from outside the Narrows, 1798. (British Museum)

What documentary evidence we have of the events is from the reports and letters of government officials and military men; there is nothing at all from the United Irishmen. But it seems certain that they were well organised in those outports and harbours around the coast of Newfoundland where the Irish predominated. The great majority of the 3,500 inhabitants of St John's in 1800 were Irish, and since the fencibles were recruited locally, most were also Irish. The authorities were not sure how loyal they would be in the event of any attack from French forces, with whom Britain was then at war, and there had been earlier evidence of discontent among the garrison in St John's which caused them further unease.

David Webber, historian of the Royal Newfoundland Regiment of Fencibles, emphasised that while conditions for the majority of ordinary people were appalling then and later, they were particularly difficult for the Irish. Popery or 'penal' laws, which restricted the social and religious activities of Catholics in Ireland and Britain, were implemented against the Irish in Newfoundland as well.

There can be no doubt that the existing social structure in the colony had already alienated the Irish from the Crown. There were many contributing factors: the poor living conditions of the troops, the near slavery of the fishermen and labourers who were kept in debt by their employers year after year, the denial of religious and political freedoms, the laws which forbade the free movement of the inhabitants, and a host of other pieces of legislation which made any chance of betterment of the poor impossible.

The vast majority of the Irish in Newfoundland came from within a thirty-mile radius of Waterford city, and thousands of young men from the area went to Newfoundland in the spring and returned the following autumn. It is safe to assume therefore that many of the Irish of St John's and soldiers in the garrison had become acquainted with the twin aims of the United Irishmen of parliamentary reform and Catholic emancipation in Ireland.

General John Skerrett, the commander of the troops in St John's since May 1799, had served in the 1798 rebellion in Ireland, and in his correspondence was inclined to exaggerate the threat from the Irish in Newfoundland. But if we are to believe his version of events, the United Irishmen were organised on the island in 1798. The duke of Kent, commander of the British forces in British North America, was based in Halifax, Nova Scotia, and Skerrett wrote to him a week after the attempted rising of April 1800: 'In 1798 they [the United Irishmen in St John's] had their Directory of five'. In any case, by the winter of 1799, it seems certain that the United Irishmen were organising on the island, and plans were being laid for a rising of some sort the following spring.

In the summer of 1799 Governor Waldegrave wrote to the duke of Portland expressing his misgivings about the Newfoundland Regiment of Fencibles. His fear was that they could not be depended upon in the event of an attack by the French: 'Your grace is well acquainted that the whole of these are of the Roman Catholic persuasion. As the Royal Newfoundland Regiment had been raised in the island, it is needless of me to endeavour to point out the small proportion the native English bear to the Irish in this body of men. I think it necessary to mention this circumstance, in order to show your grace how little dependence could be placed on the military in case of any civil commotion in the town of St John's'.

Several people who had been caught up in the terrible events of 1798 in Ireland sought refuge in Newfoundland, availing of an easy escape route through ports like New Ross and Waterford. General Skerrett claimed he recognised forty of those whom he alleged were recruiting members for the United Irishmen in St John's, and he went on to talk of the events leading up to the rising: 'The most ardent missionary to this place was an intriguing priest, Father John, a man of boisterous eloquence endowed with abundant [sic] of talent to do the utmost detriment to society'. Skerrett claimed that after his service in the rebellion in Ireland he arrived in St John's and found Father John 'with forty United men that he [Skerrett] had sent to New Geneva Barracks in Waterford to be transported for their revolutionary impiety. They bribed their way out of prison. They soon spread disruption in Newfoundland and caused the revolution in the garrison.

But Skerrett always liked to paint as dark a picture as possible, overstating the case in order to boost his own standing with the colonial authorities, and there is no record of his having arrested any of these alleged United Irishmen either before or after the attempted rising; nor is there any record of a priest called Fr. John in St John's at the time.

In any case, Bishop O'Donel (an Irish-speaking Franciscan from Tipperary) would never have tolerated any member of his clergy getting involved in anything that smacked of rebellion or sedition. Skerrett leaves us in no doubt as to where O'Donel's loyalty lay: 'I have had frequent communication with [O'Donel]. He says if there is danger in the United People, it is with this regiment…At one time from the dissolute manners of his people he lost all confidence with them and he was preparing to leave the island'.

It was with very good reason that Skerrett described O'Donel in the same letter as 'a very valuable man', because when the Bishop heard about the plot, the general was the one he informed about the plan. It was widely believed that O'Donel learned about it from a woman in confession. O'Donel's mentor in Ireland was Dr. John Troy, the Archbishop of Dublin, and like him, he had an absolute horror of French revolutionary ideas.

Documentary evidence of what took place in April 1800 is scarce, but from what we do know, it is evident that there were United Irishmen not only in St John's and the Newfoundland Regiment of Fencibles, but in several outports along the coast. In a letter to Governor Waldegrave in July 1800, the chief justice of Newfoundland, Johnathan Ogden, stated that there were four hundred men in St John's who were 'privy to this business'. He added that most of the men in those outports where the Irish predominated had taken the United oath. Skerrett confirmed Ogden's view of the numbers involved and added that it was these same people and not the men in the regiment that were behind the plot: 'The management of this conspiracy appears to have been under the direction of the same united men in town, and is of greater extent than I at first viewed it. If I was at this moment empowered to declare martial law, I would say that the standard of rebellion was erected in this Island. The Magistrates are fearful to do their duty, and the United villains are no longer restrained by fear, from the fullest conviction that they will be supported by many of the military'.

In that same letter the general stated that he was forced to strengthen the garrison in the town of Placentia, seventy-five miles south-west of St John's, 'as the United men there have been destroying houses and plundering the well affected'. It is worth noting that the most important merchant in Placentia at that time was Pierce Sweetman in whose family home at Newbawn, County Wexford, the 1798 Wexford insurgent leaders, Bagenal Harvey, John Colclough, Michael and Matthew Furlong and others—according to Sweetman family tradition—prepared for the battle of Ross. In his *Personal narrative* (1832)

33. United Irish badge.

Thomas Cloney, who took a leading part in the battle, states that they returned to the house when it was all over.

In another letter to the duke a couple of days later, Skerrett provided the additional information that many were supportive of the planned rising. He

34. Dr James Louis
    O'Donel, Catholic
    Bishop of St John's –
    from the British
    government's point
    of view 'a very
    valuable man'. (Roman
    Catholic Episcopal
    Corporation)

was convinced that there was a connection between the attempted rising in St John's and the immigration of United Irishmen after 1798. In his 1863 history of Newfoundland, Charles Pedley goes even further and states that the United Irishmen in Ireland were behind the plot and that this was set in motion some time before the rebellion in Ireland: 'This conspiracy seems to have been secretly working for some time, suggested, as was given in evidence afterwards by one implicated in the plot, by a communication from Ireland, where was organising the movement which led to the rebellion of 1798'.

The man who was 'implicated in the plot' was Nicholas McDonald, and apart from three United Irishmen who were hanged in Halifax, his is the only name we have of those arrested following the failed rising. We know nothing of his background or what became of him afterwards. Pedley noted that:

In St John's an association of United Irishmen had been formed, the members of which were leagued together by an oath. The terms of the oath were very general, as setting forth the objects of the association, so far as these were communicated to the majority of the members.

From the evidence of Nicholas M'Donald [sic], who himself had been sworn, it appears to have consisted of three parts. They are thus stated by him before the court martial:-

1st. 'By the almighty powers above, I do persevere to join the Irishmen in this place'—then he kissed the book.

2nd. 'I do persevere never to divulge the secrets made known to me'—kissed the book.

3rd. 'I do persevere to aid and assist the heads of the same, of any religion'—kissed the book. The last clause was probably directed to meet the case of such of the leaders as were not of the Catholic pale.

McDonald also said that the members used signs and passes to identify themselves, and he stated that there were about 400 men in the town who were involved in the organisation. The success of the whole venture, he said, depended on the participation of the Newfoundland Fencibles, and the United Irishmen in town were quite anxious about this; however, as Pedley says, they need not have worried, because the soldiers had their own grievances, and 'were only too likely to sympathise with the social and religious feelings of that body'.

Most of the information we have on the events of late April 1800 comes from the reports of General Skerrett and one or two other officials. Apart from the small amount of evidence given by Nicholas McDonald, there is nothing at all available from the United Irishmen; nor can we be sure how reliable McDonald's statements were.

The rising was set for Sunday 20 April, when soldiers and officers were at their religious services—'English to church, Irish to chapel' was how one officer described it. This afforded the disaffected soldiers the best opportunity of surprise because officers and soldiers were forbidden to carry their arms to divine service. According to Skerrett the plan was to massacre all the officers and the Protestant merchants in the town. Pedley added that 'should the work be thus successfully inaugurated at St John's, this was to be the signal for its reproduction throughout those districts in the colony where the conspirators were in sufficient force.

However, Skerrett and his officers, being forewarned, cancelled church services and the garrison was put on parade. The United Irish leaders, realising that the authorities had tumbled to their plans, decided to seize the town a few days later, commandeer a vessel, and make their escape to the United States.

On the following Thursday evening, 24 April, a Sergeant Kelly and twelve of the regiment deserted their posts on Signal Hill above the harbour of St John's, and at the same time, six members of the Royal Artillery at Fort Townshend above the town, left their posts and headed for a powder shed behind the fort. They were all armed and were to be joined there by thirty more soldiers—'all of them United

35. St John's from a watercolour by R.P. Brenton. Fort Townshend is above the town. Just above the ship moored on the left is the Catholic chapel and the residence of Bishop O'Donel. (Public Archives of Canada)

men'. But they were captured before they got very far. Shortly afterwards, three others were seized, four more surrendered, and the rest made for the woods.

In one of his reports, written shortly afterwards, Skerrett claimed that some of the soldiers who deserted their posts fired at those who were after them, and that 'the conspiracy was under the leadership of some united men in town, aided by that wretch James Murphy and it is of greater extent than I at first viewed it...we are now surrounded by traitors'. He said that 'James Murphy has had correspondence with the united men to the southward'. It seems that Sergeant Kelly and Murphy managed to escape.

According to Skerrett, the sheriff of St John's was afraid that efforts might be made to rescue the prisoners, and perhaps it was for this reason that he hurriedly tried them. Five were immediately hanged and eleven were sent to Halifax, Nova Scotia, in chains. On the morning of 1 July 1800, three of these eleven were hanged: Garret Fitzgerald, Pierce Ivory and Edward Power; the rest were sentenced to penal servitude for life.

Cyril Byrne is of the opinion that the authorities were at fault for appointing Skerrett as head of the army in Newfoundland, and that perhaps it was a calculated move on their part to use his experience in Ireland to check any attempts at a similar rising in Newfoundland. Was it merely ineptness on the part of the government, or was it deliberately intended as a provocation to goad the United Irishmen in St John's into open rebellion? Skerrett was colonel of the Durham Fencibles who fought at the battle of Arklow, on 9 June 1798, and his gunners were credited with the killing of Fr. Michael Murphy who was charging at the head of his men in a last desperate attempt to take the town. Pedley takes a similar view, stating that many of those Irish who found refuge in Newfoundland following the 1798 rebellion in Ireland, were 'exasperated by defeat' and their presence in St John's 'added fuel to the fire'.

After six years in the lonely outpost of Newfoundland, Skerrett was still 'crying wolf' in his letters to London. On 28 May 1805, he asked for more money to help with his expenses, and said that he had 'forced loyalty in the midst of 50,000 United Irishmen, by crushing rebellious propensities, insurrection and mutiny in the troops'. There were hardly more than 25,000 people on the whole of the island at the time!

It is interesting to note that Dr. O'Donel, too, was concerned about money that same year. He was thinking of retiring, and wanted to make sure that the pension of £50 that he had been awarded for his part in helping to put down the rising would continue after he stepped down. Pedley states that O'Donel wrote to the king, beseeching him to continue paying the pension after he retired from the island.

It is still not clear what precisely the United Irishmen had in mind when they planned the rising, but according to one source, their only defence at their trial was that they were dissatisfied with the authorities who had reneged on a promise to allow the soldiers of the garrison to work at the fishery that summer. It may very well have been spurred by a burning resentment following the brutal suppression of the rebellion in Ireland and the continuing unsettled conditions there.

Although the United Irishmen's attempted rising in 1800 failed, it did not stifle Catholic agitation for equality and reform. On the contrary, Irish Catholics were to the fore in seeking self–government for Newfoundland. According to Raymond Lahey, the irony of it all was that the intervention of Bishop O'Donel enhanced the standing of the Catholic church in the community, and won it the favour of an appreciative government: 'Indeed, his handling of the affair cemented an alliance between the government of Newfoundland and the Roman Catholic clergy that was to endure well into the future. This co-operation worked to mutual advantage'.

Chapter 9

Emigrant letters:
'I take up my pen to write these few lines'

David Fitzpatrick

The uses of literacy, the ability to read and write, are central to the construction of popular culture. Cultural historians have long been engrossed with the reading habits of ordinary people, hoping to find clues to their knowledge, beliefs, expectations and fantasies. Yet the forms and functions of popular writing have been largely ignored. This neglect is perhaps attributable to problems of evidence. A single chap-book may illuminate the mentality of a thousand readers, whereas a thousand letters may fail to reveal the intentions of a single writer. Even so, the personal letter offers a powerful challenge to historians concerned with the uses of the written word for those with rudimentary education. Until relatively recently, the scarcity of accessible plebeian letters provided a plausible excuse for inactivity. This excuse has been undermined by the growing interest of descendants in the private writings of their ancestors. The value of old letters, once appreciated only by stamp-collectors, has attracted particular attention from the armies of 'roots-hunters' from America and Australasia, who swarm every summer over the libraries of Europe and Ireland. Their efforts have uncovered tens of thousands of private letters, sent or received by the emigrants of the last century or so. Some of these documents have been deposited in archives, though many remain in private possession. A couple of thousand letters survive to represent the Irish in Australia, providing the basis for what follows.

Historians of emigration were, understandably, among the first to edit or extract plebeian letters. In addition to generating many compilations by family historians, emigrant letters have been exploited by a distinguished line of scholars, stretching from William Thomas and Florian Znaniecki to Kerby Miller and Patrick O'Farrell. With few exceptions, these studies have used letters purely as a source of 'factual' illustration, the often quaint phraseology providing an additional gloss of authenticity by comparison with the newspaper report or emigrant manual. The letters have been allowed to 'speak for themselves', offering seemingly direct access to personal experience as described for an intimate circle. Even Miller and O'Farrell, two of the finest

36. *The Bushman's Dream* 1869 by Thomas Selby Cousins. (Courtesy of National Library of Australia)

historians of Irish emigration, have scarcely concerned themselves with the details of personal or local background. Still less interest has been expressed in the functions of letter-writing or the genres of 'epistolary discourse', though Stephen Fender has belatedly alerted literary critics to the distinctive idiom and rhetoric of emigrant letters.

Should letters be left to 'speak for themselves'? Consider this message from Isabella Wyly in Adelaide to the widow of her brother Thomas in Newry, sent in about December 1857: 'I think I told you before that I had become quite a Wesleyan I hope not in Name only but in heart. I have been one now for 4 years and I hope I shall Dye one, and I trust a Good one. But it does not mater what you ar by Name as long as you belong to that one church that is the church of God, and I hope we are all united to that one'. The only 'fact' conveyed by this passage is an emigrant's conversion from an unrevealed denomination. That bare fact takes on richer meaning when we investigate Isabella's background. Her parents were lapsed Quakers who had been converted to the Church of Ireland. A sister had caused a sensation in 1841 by eloping to the Presentation convent at George's Hill, Dublin, only to be abducted by brother Thomas in company with the firebrand preacher, T. D. ('Trash') Gregg. Conversions were clearly a delicate matter in the Wyly family. Isabella's change of affiliation should also be set in the unique context of South Australia, that 'paradise of dissent', where Wesleyanism was the dominant faith among the oligarchy. Furthermore, the passage may have fulfilled a hidden function by preparing the Irish Wylys for Isabella's future marriage to her Wesleyan employer. Finally, the form of the letter invites analysis, in its use of conventional phrases naively strung together and imperfectly spelt. Indeed, the 'bare facts' are perhaps the least interesting element of emigrant letters.

Making sense of emigrant correspondence is a daunting undertaking. The construction of my book, *Oceans of Consolation*, indicates one strategy for teasing out personal meanings without abandoning the quest for a general analysis of the migratory experience. The book included the full and undoctored text of fourteen sequences, covering the period 1843-1906 and containing over a hundred letters, out of the thousands that survive and the millions that must have been written. Many of these letters were located through public appeals in both Ireland and Australia. Clearly, no such selection should be presented as a 'sample', either of letter-writers or of the whole body of Irish-Australian emigrants. Instead, I sought out the atypical minority of letters by the unlettered. My selection is dominated by Catholics, the rural poor and the ill-educated, matching their predominance among Irish emigrants. Letters from home were given no less prominence than those sent by emigrants, since these accounts of changing conditions in Ireland offer fascinating insight into Irish mentality. Despite the shortage of surviving letters by women, these account for one selection in three. Although these individual voices cannot speak for the silent thousands, they address problems of separation and adjustment that must have confronted innumerable families splintered by migration.

Each sequence is accompanied by a commentary, reconstructing the family and local contexts in both Ireland and Australia. Using the finding aids and techniques developed by family historians, I was able to follow the paths of migration in some detail. It is heartening to discover that almost every emigrant correspondent, however obscure, left some traces in the records of both countries. My intention was to allow the reader to eavesdrop on these semi-private conversations, filling in some of the silences and decoding inexplicit messages. We also learn something about those receiving the letters, making up for the predictable loss of one side of almost every correspondence. On occasion, the background research provided a 'key' to otherwise perplexing passages (convict origins, or a mixed marriage). By relating the letters to the lives of their writers, I have tried to illustrate the ulterior uses of 'factual' statements. Seemingly objective accounts of economic conditions in Australia, or the prospects of particular classes, may often be interpreted as tactical statements, intended to encourage or discourage further migration by particular relations or neighbours.

The interpretation of letters demands close attention to their intended functions. French historians have rightly emphasised the need to define the 'space' within which correspondence is conducted. Though personal and sometimes intimate in tone, it is evident that these letters were collaborative rather than strictly private. Messages were sent to a vast range of relations and neighbours, and writers were conscious that their words would be quite widely broadcast. This is confirmed by references to other people's letters, which were often cited in order to goad a correspondent to write more often, send more money, or check some dubious report. The act of writing, too, was often collaborative. Some letters have several signatories, and others were inscribed by an amanuensis—often the sender's better-educated son or daughter. The possibility of dictation enabled many of the sub-literate to overcome the most obvious impediment to letter-writing. Thus Irish-Australian letters typically had the somewhat guarded character of semi-private rather than private communications. Even when the soul was bared, it was done self-consciously before a mixed audience.

A central function of emigrant correspondence was to assert the writer's continuing stake in the ever-dispersing networks stretching out from 'home'. The emigrant used words to maintain emotional, social and economic ties, in defiance of physical separation. The untutored eloquence and rhetorical prowess of many Irish writers enabled them both to offer and solicit consolation, and to reinforce affection, love and sympathy. Letters were used to influence home decisions, to tease out news of family enterprises, and above all to regulate future emigration. Parents in Ireland, sometimes no less isolated than their

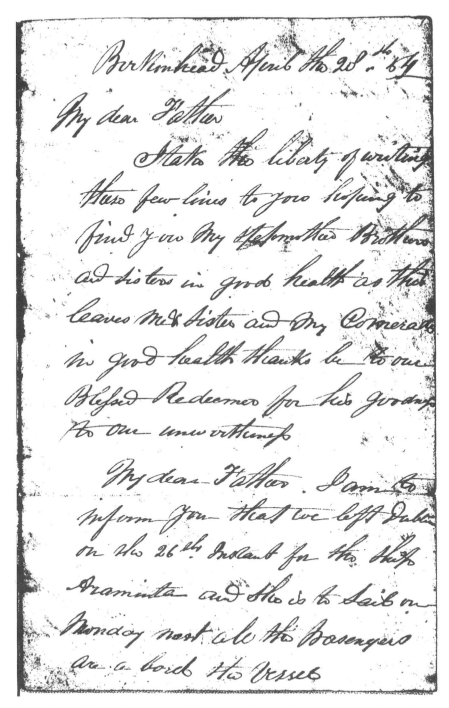

37. Michael Normile's farewell letter to Clare before leaving for New South
    Wales, 28 April 1854. (Courtesy of Miss M.K. Normoyle)

emigrant children, likewise interfered with decisions in Australia. The traffic in money, as well as moral suasion, occurred in both directions. The best-documented practical consequence of correspondence was the organisation of further movement, and letters provide unrivalled insight into the construction of 'chain' migration. The Australian nomination system, whereby free passages were provided on payment of a non-refundable deposit by a colonial resident, gave emigrants particular power over the selection of successors. We are able to follow the often elaborate process of negotiation, chart the arrival and settlement of nominated emigrants, and trace their own subsequent nominations. On the basis of names given in letters, collated with official documents, we can even reconstruct and map the 'social fields' of writers in both Ireland and Australia. The much-despised 'rosters' of names thus provide a powerful tool for defining the networks within which fractured families subsisted.

The forms and idioms of emigrant letters present a tantalising challenge to future students of popular discourse. The plebeian letter of the nineteenth century was far more measured and ceremonious than the casual and ephemeral messages exchanged by moderners over telephone or email. This was partly due to the expense and sluggishness of the mails, although these constraints changed dramatically over the century. In the later 1830s, a single 'ship' letter sent between inland New South Wales and Clare would have cost over half a

38. News from Australia (1864) by Geoge Baxter. (Courtesy National Library of Australia)

crown, equivalent to several days' earnings for an Irish labourer. By 1854, the basic rate for half an ounce was down to sixpence, falling to fourpence in 1889, twopence ha'penny in 1891, and only a penny by the early twentieth century. Transit times also declined steeply, from up to five months in the 1840s to three in the following decades, two by 1860, and four or five weeks by the late Victorian period. Despite these advances, the transmission of a letter was still a major enterprise in the 1880s. The writer was responding to outdated news and could not expect a reply for several months, so facing an exaggerated case of what discourse specialists term the 'paradox of temporal polyvalence': the need to imagine oneself in several periods, as well as places, at once. Instead of jotting down the day's events, the writer had to combine current observation with both remembrance and prediction. Writers were also aware that there was no alternative means for maintaining active contact between members of separated families, except in the unusual event of a return to Ireland. It is scarcely surprising that most letter-writers took great pains to find appropriately memorable phrases, and seldom chattered about trivia.

The seriousness of letters is reflected in their idiom, most strikingly in the elaborate salutations. Here is a characteristic example: 'I take up my pen to write these few lines to you hoping to find you and all your family in good health as this leaves us all at present thank god'. The writer offers an evocation of the act of writing, ritualised references to good health (in other cases immediately followed by details of illness or death), and thanksgiving. This type of salutation was used in letters from both Australia and Ireland and corresponds closely with phrases regarded as a 'standing joke' by the Irish Folklore Commission's aged informants in the 1950s. In this and other respects, the idiom of Irish-Australian letters was probably indistinguishable from the Irish-American case, although this has yet to be demonstrated. No positive model has been found in composition exercises or letter-writing manuals, suggesting that the formal phrases of plebeian correspondence developed autonomously, in the manner of a spoken dialect. The written and spoken courtesies of rural Ireland were parallel but distinct, verbal counterparts being 'God save all here', or 'I am indeed, thanks be to God for all'. Yet similar ceremonies of salutation occurred far beyond Ireland, being found in the Polish 'bowing letter' and also in 'letter-writing as practised by uneducated persons' in England—according to a manual of 1856. Its writer parodied the vulgar form: 'This comes hopping to find you all well, as it leaves us at present, thank God for it'; and, by way of variation, 'I take up my pen to write you these few lines'.

Irish-Australian letters are peppered with proverbs and grandiloquent phrases, sometimes with comic effect: 'I take up my old quill once more to reply to your welcome letter . . . and to congrulate you on your instalation in your new habiation.' Yet these flourishes are interspersed with long passages of narrative, and commentary, often achieving the effect of informal chat. Many influences may be traced in the informal idiom: pet names and other private family forms; local dialect (scarcely ever tinged with an Australian accent); and the more stilted phraseology of newspapers or sermons. Many writers actually pictured themselves as chatting rather than inscribing: 'I must soon quit talking to yous'; 'I will draw this long yarn to a close'; 'I for once in 12 mounths sit to have a few words of conversation with you'; 'actualy my Dear Father I fancy I am speaking to you verbaly while I am writing this scroll to you but my grife I am not'. In their simulation of chat, the writers were unwittingly following the medieval rules of the *Ars Dictaminis*, with its juxtaposition of the formal *salutatio* with the proverbial *exordium* and the conversational *narratio*. Bolognese rhetoricians and Irish peasants hit upon similar designs, calculated yet flexible, whereby courtesy and intimacy worked in harness to advance the writer's interests.

The study of form and function, fascinating though it seems, must remain subsidiary to the analysis of content. By elucidating the rhetorical structures and personal contexts of letters, the historian is enabled to offer a more reliable interpretation of the expressed facts and opinions. In *Oceans of Consolation*, I synthesised relevant extracts from all of the selected letters under many hundreds of categories, so constructing an orchestrated (if discordant) version of the individual voices. The thematic analysis is intended to provide a comprehensive and balanced report of the chosen correspondence, without purporting to unveil the collective mentality of all correspondents, emigrants, or Irish 'peasants'. Perhaps its most valuable function is to chart the immense range of sometimes unexpected Irish responses to migration, life in Australia, and life at home.

The letters reveal startling complexity in the stratagems by which emigration was organised. Emigrants gave up-to-date and accurate guidance on the relative provision of assistance in different colonies, advised on outfit and provisions for the voyage, and specified the classes best fitted for Australian conditions. Writers from Ireland played an active role in the selection of emigrants, sometimes using their children in Australia as agents by sending them the sums required for nomination. One settler on the Victorian goldfields combined with a friend in Grey Abbey, County Down, to organise a succession of emigrant passages involving a convoluted network of evangelical Protestants. The letters also document the complexity of onward migration, and the cosmopolitanism of the nineteenth-century Irish. Virtually every sequence referred to acquaintances or relations in the United States, with connections as far afield as China and South America. The mental map of the correspondents thus extended far beyond Ireland and Australia.

Lack of parochialism is also indicated by the manner in which correspondents treated conditions in the two countries. The geographical displacement of writer and reader ensured that most observations about local conditions evoked a comparison, explicit or implicit, with the other country. Writers in Ireland

Clougheen Decr 23rd 69

My Dear Children.

It is with Joy we received
Year Joint and welcome letter
which gives us an Account of your
being in good health. And united
in Marrage as a loveing Couple
which all the friends and Neighbours
were glad of. Dear Margaret your
Mama and I am well pleased
with your Choice, and though
you did not acquaint us of it previous to your Marrage, we are well
pleased with your Choice as being
in the hands of a good Mam and
neighbours Child we now give
ye Our Blessing from Our heart
and will not forget praying

39. Pat Carroll's letter from Clare to his daughter and son-in-law in Victoria,
    23 December 1869. (Courtesy of Mrs P.G. Nottle)

struggled to imagine Australian life, and also to persuade those in Australia that Ireland too was changing rapidly. The images of both environments were on balance positive, and Irish writers took care to boast of post-Famine improvements in the economy, social conditions, and even the weather. Those in the colonies often contrasted the two cultures, pitting the simple comforts and remembered cheeriness of Irish life with the crass appeal of money-crazed Australia. Indeed, the student of these letters is confronted by two disparate prescriptions for human happiness, often coexisting in a single mind. In New South Wales, Michael Normile ruminated that 'I might be a wealthier man than what I am at presant If I did go to the wild country to live and live there like wild cattle'. Instead, he had sacrificed quick riches for Irish-style snugness: 'I did not choose to go far away. I am near the priest & church and religion I have plenty as yet thank God.' Unlike Fender's English writers, extolling the virtues of America while decrying 'old world' ways, the Irish-Australian dialogue evinced qualified admiration for both ways of life.

Even so, there was only slight ambiguity about the location of 'home'. The reiteration of this word invites a statistical analysis of its connotations, ranging from house to neighbourhood and nation, straying from Ireland to Australia or even to 'our heavenly home'. This most highly charged of words was seldom applied to Australia, except in the bare sense of a place or dwelling. When set in Ireland, it provided the focus for many an expression of nostalgia, regret, or affection. No doubt, as those feelings receded, correspondence lapsed. The study of letters illuminates the experience of migration in the transitional phase between displacement and disconnection. The silence following each final letter still defies interpretation.

Chapter 10

Secret diasporas:
the Irish in Latin America and the Caribbean

Edmundo Murray

The legendary visit of St Brendan to Mexico in the sixth century—and his resemblance to the Aztec creator-god Quetzacóatl—may have been mythical, but it is an indication of the mystery and sense of exceptionality surrounding relations between Ireland and Latin America. Yet, just like the rest of the diaspora, the Irish in Latin America hoped to improve their lot in military, business, religious or social ways. Less numerous than their compatriots in North America, Britain or Australia, Irish missionaries, soldiers, merchants, teachers, farmers and others who settled in the region left their traces, or re-emigrated to other parts of the world.

The number of Irish who decided on Latin America as their temporary or permanent home is still a matter of debate among scholars. Argentina and Uruguay alone received approximately 50,000 Irish-born immigrants. Thousands more were scattered in the Caribbean, Brazil, Venezuela and Mexico as a result of military operations, trade and colonisation schemes. The rate of re-emigration within the Americas and to Australia, Britain or back to Ireland was high, yet similar to that of other immigrant communities.

Migration to Latin America was initially an extension of the Iberian dimension of the Irish diaspora. The first recorded Irish arrivals there were those of Juan and Tomás Farrel, who accompanied Pedro de Mendoza to found Buenos Aires in the Río de la Plata region in 1536. The early Irish presence in Latin America has been connected with traditional links between the Irish in Britain, Spain and Portugal.

Among the missionaries was the Jesuit Thomas Field, born in Limerick, who entered the Order in Rome and arrived in Brazil in 1577. With two other Jesuits, he went to Paraguay and established missions among the Guaraní people. Other priests were born in Spain or Portugal of Irish parents, and were engaged by the Jesuits and Franciscans to mission in Latin America because they spoke English. Thus they could work not only to protect the native populations from Protestant English and Dutch colonisers, but also to convert the 'heretics' themselves.

40. Rubens' *Portrait of a Young Captain*, reputedly William Lamport from Wexford, an early proponent of Mexican independence and known locally as Guillén Lombardo. He was jailed in October 1642 and died in prison in 1659. (Timken Museum of Art, San Diego)

In *circa* 1612 the brothers Philip and James Purcell established a plantation in Forte de Tauregue, on the mouth of the River Amazon. Huge profits were made by the colonists in tobacco, dyes and hardwoods. They were followed by Bernardo O'Brien of County Clare, who built a fort on the north bank of the Amazon and named the place Coconut Grove. Other plantations existed in Guyana and the Caribbean islands, where owners, managers, foremen and, in some cases, indentured labourers also came from Ireland. In Jamaica, Puerto Rico, St Domingue, Montserrat, St Croix and other islands, the Irish produced tobacco, sugar, coffee, cacao and cattle. In Cuba, Richard O'Farrill from Montserrat made a fortune in the slave trade, and his family became significant owners of tobacco and sugar plantations, cattle ranches, sugar mills and hundreds of slaves.

Irish soldiers were also active in the region by the end of the eighteenth century and during its various wars of independence were members of British, Spanish, Portuguese and South American armies. In the eighteenth century the Spanish regiment Ultonia, with Irish origins in Catalonia, was stationed in Mexico. In Chile, the Spanish Crown appointed Ambrose O'Higgins of County Sligo as governor, and later as viceroy of Peru. His son Bernardo would became a national hero of the Chilean struggle for independence . . . from Spain!

In 1762 the British attacked Colonia del Sacramento in Uruguay, but failed when their flagship blew up, killing several Irish soldiers. In 1806 and 1807, during the British campaigns against colonial Buenos Aires, a significant number of soldiers were Irish. The campaigns failed and the invaders were repulsed, but some of the prisoners and deserters settled and prospered in Argentina, and played a role in early migration from Westmeath to this region.

During the South American wars of independence, the Irish saw military action as legionaries in Simón Bolívar's army, and fought in Venezuela, Colombia, Panama, Ecuador, Peru and Bolivia. The Irish Legion of John Devereux, supported by Daniel O'Connell, arrived in Venezuela in 1817 but soon mutinied and was devastated by epidemics. Bolívar said he was 'pleased to be rid of these mercenaries who would do no killing until they had first been paid for it'. Other Irish soldiers fought with honour and were recognised for their gallantry, like Francis Burdett O'Connor and Daniel Florence O'Leary. In Argentina, William Brown created the navy that broke the Spanish blockade, and John Thomond O'Brien engaged in battle in Chile and Peru. Other Irishmen who fought for the new republics were Thomas Charles Wright of Drogheda, Peter Campbell of Tipperary, Patricio Lynch (a naval hero in Chile), Diago Nicolau Keating, Diago O'Grady and Jorge Cowan, who served in Brazilian armies.

The most celebrated Irish military exploit in Latin America was that of the Batallón San Patricio of the Mexican army against the United States in 1846–48. Led by John O'Reilly of Clifden, County Galway, hundreds of Irish and other

US soldiers deserted to the Mexican side and fought under a green banner with an Irish harp and shamrock. The 'San Patricios' distinguished themselves in the battles of Buena Vista and Churubusco. At the end of the war they were captured and court-martialled, and thirty were hanged. Their bravery is widely known among Mexicans today. Understandably, they were regarded as traitors in the US.

From Veracruz in Mexico, where the Murphy family traded fruit, arms and slaves, to the wool-exporters in southernmost Punta Arenas, Irish business people of all trades and ranks were present in the major ports and cities of Latin America.

In 1822 there were 3,500 *ingleses* (British and Irish) in Buenos Aires, where they made up the majority of foreigners who benefited from the free trade treaty signed with Britain in 1824. Merchants traded for silver, *maté* (a type of beverage), hides, talon and jerked beef. King's County-born Thomas Armstrong led the Irish business community from its early stages in the 1830s until his death in 1875. Thomas O'Gorman, Patrick Lynch and Peter Sheridan were also prominent members of the business community. Other Irish people were employed by British firms, like William Mooney and Patrick Bookey of County Westmeath, and Patrick Brown and James Pettit of Wexford. They were the initiators of early immigration chains from those counties to Argentina and Uruguay. Moreover, there were Irish-born stevedores and labourers in the meat-curing establishments.

From the 1850s, Irish merchants were established in Rio de Janeiro, Mexico, the West Indies and on the Pacific coast. In Valparaíso, Chile, the Irish and British contributed to business and social life. In Bolivia, Peru and Ecuador they opened trading houses and were involved in shipping and mining businesses. William Russell Grace of Cork became one of the most prominent businessmen in the Americas, with interests in almost all South American countries and in the US.

Irish colonies in Latin America were conceived to populate deserted areas and to *whiten* the native population. In the 1840s a 'New Ireland' in California was planned by Fr Eugene McNamara of County Clare. His projected colony was approved by the Mexican authorities but collapsed when the US annexed California from Mexico. William Cotter, an Irish officer serving in the Brazilian army, recruited some 3,000 people in Cork. When they arrived at Rio de Janeiro they were abandoned on the streets and mutinied. Most left Brazil but some went on to form a colony in Pernambuco.

Irish *empresarios* (entrepreneurs) established successful settlements in Mexican Texas, where settlers were brought from Wexford to establish colonies in Refugio and San Patricio on the Gulf Coast. They perceived themselves as Mexican through marriage, commercial contacts and as Spanish speakers. During the Texas revolution some of the Irish were loyal to the Mexican government and established successful relations with *vaquero* neighbours, from whom they

41. Celebration of St Patrick's Day, 1922, at Arrecifes in the north-west of Buenos Aires province. (Centro Argentino Irlandés de San Pedro)

learned the basics of the cattle business. Other Irish settlements started in the Chaco region of Paraguay, Osorno in southern Chile, and in Patagonia.

The last Irish colony was established near Bahía Blanca, Argentina, with 700 passengers from the steamer *Dresden*, which sailed from Cork in 1889. They were part of a larger immigration scheme planned by the Argentine government and leaders of the Irish-Argentine community. Agents working out of Dublin and Cork convinced thousands of destitute people to travel to Argentina with false promises. In what later became notorious as the 'Dresden affair', many died—especially children—or re-emigrated to other destinations.

In 1835 some 400 Irish workers were hired in New York and laboured in brutal conditions to open the 'sugar railroad' between Havana and Güines. Workers from the Canary Islands and Ireland—described by the royal council in Havana as 'worthless, lazy, disease-ridden drunkards'—were involved in the first recorded strike in Cuba. Likewise, the Irish workers in the multinational force on the Panama railroad between Colón and Panamá were deceived and abused. Feuds arose between the Irish and workers from other places. No other nationality displayed so much animosity towards people of darker skin and foreign ways as the Irish, and therefore the Chinese camp was relocated as far away from them as possible.

Many prosperous Irish-Argentine families perceived themselves as *ingleses* and their identity tended towards British rather than Irish traditions. In contrast, the poorer classes, made up of countryside labourers, urban servants and low-rank employees, were attracted by Irish nationalist appeals from the Catholic Church. The Irish-owned newspapers in Buenos Aires, *The Standard* and *The Southern Cross*, polarised the interests of these distinct identities.

The most flourishing Irish rural settlements in the region grew up in the Argentine and Uruguayan Pampas. The successful integration of the immigrants into the wool production cycle was followed by spontaneous networks attracting family members, neighbours and friends from Ireland. Between 1830 and 1930 about 50,000 emigrants went to Argentina. One half returned to Ireland or re-emigrated to other places, but the other half formed the Irish-Argentine community. The success ratio of the latter group, measured by access to landownership, was disproportionate compared to the Irish diaspora in other destinations (though French-Basque and Catalan immigrants in Argentina in the same period were equally successful).

Most of the emigrants were the sons (and later the daughters) of middle-sized farmers from Westmeath, Longford, Offaly and Wexford, though there were smaller groups from Dublin, Cork and Clare. They nurtured the dream of owning 2,000 hectares in South America instead of being tenants of 20 hectares in Ireland. In the Pampas they were hired by ranchers to look after their sheep, and some managed to acquire land thanks to the increase in wool prices between 1830 and 1880, together with convenient agreements for half or third of the produce in wool and lambs. A few purchased large tracts of land from the government in areas gained from the indigenous peoples. The vast majority, however, were ranch hands and labourers, and could never purchase land. Stories circulated in Ireland of poor emigrants who became wealthy landowners in South America. These stories, frequently exaggerated, were sometimes fuelled by those who failed to settle successfully in Argentina but could not admit to failure back home.

The 'Dresden affair' and other failures ended further projects to attract Irish immigrants. A small but continuous flow arrived from Belfast, Cork, Dublin and Limerick, some of them from a Protestant background. Skilled workers were hired by railway companies, banks or meat-packing plants in Argentina. After the First World War, in which some Irish-Argentines fought in British regiments, more arrived during the Irish Civil War. Financial crisis and catastrophe in Europe were serious barriers to emigration, and consequently Irish arrivals in Argentina virtually came to a halt after 1930.

The newly-rich Irish families did not wish to be perceived by the Anglophile Argentine elite as belonging to the same circles as their poorer relatives in Ireland. A social gap arose between the Irish in Argentina and the Irish in Ireland, and weakened the links between both communities (even within the same families). In other Latin American countries the British predominance gradually gave way to US businesses. By the 1920s most of the families with Irish surnames in Latin America were considered—and considered themselves—to be Brazilians, Chileans, Mexicans and so on, rather than Irish.

The first Irish diplomatic envoy to Latin America was Argentine-born Éamonn Bulfin, who established a contact network in South America and started an Irish fund in support of the underground Irish republic in 1921. By that time two of Ireland's eight republican envoys were based in Latin America. Formal diplomatic relations with the region started in 1947 with the opening of a mission in Buenos Aires, followed by Brazil and Mexico in 1975 and 1977 respectively.

The most efficient Irish representatives in Latin America have been religious missionaries. Most knowledge of Latin America in Ireland is derived from missionary news circulated through churches. The pioneering work of Fr Anthony Fahy and other Irish chaplains in nineteenth-century South America was followed by religious orders. The Sisters of Mercy and the Passionist and Pallotine fathers served the Irish community in remote regions. Irish missionary work with Latin Americans started when the Columbans opened parishes in Peru and Chile in 1952. The Legion of Mary followed in Colombia and attracted other orders that established missions from El Salvador to southern Chile.

In a process that ended with the Falklands (Malvinas) War of 1982, the Irish in Latin America gradually came to perceive themselves as Argentines,

42. Wheat-threshing at the Youngs ranch in Orlando, February 1938. Irish-Argentinian landowners such as the Youngs hired contractors like Aleotti Formigoni (right), who owned the steam-powered threshing machine. (Centro Argentino Irlandés de San Pedro)

Brazilians or Mexicans with Irish family names. Present-day Latin Americans with an Irish background are estimated at *circa* 500,000, and most live in Argentina. The vast majority do not speak English nor keep the traditions brought from Ireland by their ancestors. Inter-community marriage during the twentieth century has allowed most of the families to assert their local Latin American identities. Nevertheless, perhaps seeking recognition of their Irish identity, in 2002 a group of about 2,000 Irish-Argentines submitted a petition to the Irish minister for justice for permission to reside in Ireland. While the petition failed to obtain a favourable response, it was a demonstration that the links between Ireland and Latin America can still be reshaped to accommodate the needs of both societies.

Reversing the trend, since the late 1990s Ireland has attracted immigrants from the region. The most significant community consisted Brazilians in Counties Galway and Roscommon. Most are from the interior of the state of São Paulo and came with the experience of working in slaughterhouses in Brazil. Furthermore, embassies from Argentina, Brazil, Chile, Cuba and Mexico reinforce the relation and work to attract investment. Immigrants and diplomats act more realistically than St Brendan did in Mexico, and have created the basis for further relations between Ireland and Latin America.

43. A carnival party at Youngs ranch c. 1930s. Sara and Louise Young (with guitars) and their friends wear fancy dress representing Argentinian native women. (Centro Argentino Irlandés de San Pedro)

Chapter 11

Lifting the veil on entrepreneurial Irishwomen: running convents in nineteenth-century England and Wales

Barbara Walsh

The governing responsibilities of the mother superior of a convent, as laid down by nineteenth-century Canon Law, stated that she may 'make ordinary purchases necessary to provide shelter or clothing or which are needed for the ordinary upkeep of property. She may [perform] acts of ordinary administration . . . enter into contracts of buying and selling . . . gifts, loans, rents and all other acts of a similar nature'. In other words, a considerable amount of decision-making in financial and business matters was needed, and the women who managed religious institutions were required to have experience, skill and business acumen. References in convent annals and obituaries cite sisters who were 'endowed with great business capacity' or had 'a skill in business matters and a power of administration which astonished men of the world'.

These particular quotations relate to a couple of dynamic English-born nuns but contain sentiments which could equally be applied to hundreds, if not thousands, of Irishwomen recruited out of Ireland to join religious orders since the 1850s. In the main drawn from middle-class farming families, these young women would live out the rest of their days abroad in England, North America, Australia, Africa, India, China and elsewhere. The religious institutions of their choice in many instances did not even possess a house in Ireland, and girls set off to report to novitiates in England, or even further afield. Unaccounted for in the shadowy grey statistics that chart female emigration figures, they slipped away from these shores—for the most part never to return.

Close examination of the growth of religious orders in these islands reveals the startling fact that there were far more Roman Catholic convents in England and Wales than in Ireland by the latter half of the nineteenth century. From 1870 onwards several waves of French, German and other European communities had fled to seek sanctuary on English soil, driven there by European anti-clerical legislation, wars and other civil strife. An early exodus was triggered by the Franco-Prussian war of 1870–71, Bismarck's Kulturkampf (1871–87) and the 'Falk laws' of 1873, which sought to completely suppress the influence of

44. The Daughters of Charity of St Vincent de Paul dispensing bread in 1916. (Murtagh Collection)

the Roman Catholic church in Prussia. The trickle of exiles later became a fast-growing flow. French religious communities fell foul of Combe's educational laws of July 1904 that forbade them to teach and ordered their houses to be shut within ten years. Congregations of nursing sisters were also eventually banned from French hospitals and they, too, chose exile in due course.

The financial viability and survival of these communities' convent life in exile, however, relied very much on their ability to earn their keep as educationalists, nurses or social care workers. They also now needed many more English-speaking members. But the Catholic population of England, although increasing, was still small. The convents switched their attention to Ireland and, as one former French community put it, they set about 'gleaning from the land of St Patrick'. It was a stupendously successful tactic, as will be shown.

As the earliest influx of exiled religious communities were arriving in England, government agencies were already coping with the result of changes in the administration of the old Poor Laws. Voluntary bodies of all denominations had been gearing up to provide charitable social services and there was rising public concern over health and education issues. Institutional care and rehabilitation of those in need was a priority, and the newly arrived religious communities found themselves working at the cutting edge of the many social and economic developments taking place in Britain. In addition, the increasingly benign climate of tolerance, which had led to the English Catholic hierarchy being re-established in 1851, had brought about a flurry of parish (at that time called mission) consolidation. Spurred on by both church and government approval, convents built, administered and staffed hundreds of schools at every level of education from pre-school crèches for working mothers to coaching girls for university entrance. They provided teacher training colleges, hostels, homes and orphanages. They established and ran hospitals, asylums, institutions, organised nursing services, and a wide range of other social care. The increase in the number and expansion of religious houses was nothing short of phenomenal. Some were very large—holding perhaps upwards of ninety sisters—while others were smaller but, as a rule, accommodating not less than twelve nuns. They were soon an established presence in every corner of England and Wales.

The average Victorian, especially if non-Catholic, liked to shroud this choice of lifestyle for women in a mysterious gothic mist which hinted of nefarious intent and dark medieval practices. With newly established convent houses springing up in almost every English city and town, a great wave of alarm began to rise. Questions were asked in parliament. There was a demand for immediate legislation to provide for convent inspection and the issue became a well-aired talking-point. Public curiosity about all matters connected with nuns became obsessive. There were cartoons in *Punch*, and not for nothing was the most popular painting in the Royal Academy in 1868 a depiction of a young girl being rescued in the nick of time by a dashing medieval knight just as she was being bricked up alive in a convent wall by a coterie of evil-looking monks and nuns. Its sensational title, 'Not a whit too soon!', was guaranteed to create plenty of notice and fashionable acclaim. In 1872 a pamphlet going the rounds in London warned of 'swarms of Jesuits [attracted] to this country . . . who had got wind of a vast horde of potential recruits to Roman Catholic convents'.

The public concern at the expansion of convent life, while bordering on the hysterical, was not, however, over-imaginative in its predictions. By the 1880s there were already far more convents in England and Wales than in Ireland. By the turn of the century the pattern of growth had continued. Less than two decades into the new century, there would be twice as many convents in England as in Ireland.

In providing a response to social needs the convents had willingly engaged in hundreds of new undertakings, and their services were supported by and well used by Catholics and non-Catholics alike. But none of these activities could be developed without a large intake of new aspirants to religious life. All the convents were seeking personnel. All were recruiting heavily. In England the religious orders could, of course, tap the traditional heartlands of old English Catholicism to be found in Lancashire and parts of the north-east, in addition to drawing from the melting-pot of London. Analysis of these recruitment patterns reveals a wealth of Irish surnames and backgrounds—evidence of the Irish diaspora—also to be found in the west of Scotland. But the volume of aspirants from these sources was relatively small and unable to provide enough girls who, as nuns, could teach, nurse or tackle the social problems to be addressed.

Analysis of professed (fully accepted) membership of four religious institutions, only one of which had a house based in Ireland prior to the twentieth century, reveal that their intake over about eighty years was reliant on high numbers of Irishwomen and, in particular, on aspirants from Munster and south Leinster. A line can be drawn from Louth to Limerick to trace these sisters' birthplaces. Coincidentally, the same line also marks out the best farming land in Ireland. Poor soil, stone, bog and wild mountainside were not, it seems, fertile ground for vocations. Great swaths of Ireland accounted for barely one per cent of intake, or less. Clearly many religious institutions preferred girls drawn from solid middle-class backgrounds—the daughters of substantial farming households.

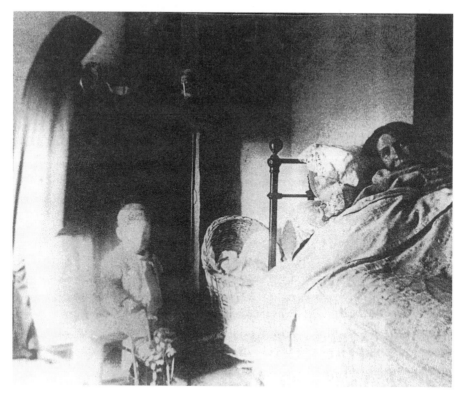

45. In attendance at a domestic sickbed – the newly arrived religious communities found themselves working at the cutting edge of the many social and economic developments taking place in Britain. (Peter Walsh)

Fortunately for the convents seeking young women at this time, many economic and social changes had deeply affected the farming families of Munster and Leinster. From the 1870s onwards, having survived the Great Famine, a new middle class of 'strong farmers', cattle-dealers and small town merchants had emerged. The gradual changes in farming practice, however, had started to erode the traditional farming role for farmers' daughters. Slowly, areas of work that had formerly been their responsibility were disappearing. Male-run creameries were taking over the milking and butter-making. The setting up of farm co-ops and the emergence of middlemen had edged into egg production and pig- and poultry-keeping. Consequently, as the convents discovered, there was a growing pool of unemployed strong farmers' daughters for the picking. Alternative off-farm employment for these girls in rural areas did not exist. Many from the larger homesteads would have been relatively well educated at the local convent school and it could be suspected that they might have thought themselves too high up the social scale of 'respectability' to have considered the possibility of emigration to seek work as domestic servants or factory hands. However, to teach, nurse or engage in social work was, by contrast, considered a very 'ladylike' and worthy occupation with status. To engage in this work, while at the same time being protected by the security of a religious habit, would have appeared very desirable, even leaving aside all the higher religious motives which undoubtedly provided a strong driving force. Census returns bear testimony to the hundreds, if not thousands, described merely as 'farmer's daughter' still living at home. For example, in County Limerick in 1901 and 1911, out of 54 farming families traced from which daughters had entered one English congregation, only two households had an alternative occupation for their girls. In one a young woman worked as a teacher; in another three sisters were seamstresses.

Family pressures brought encouragement. Manuscripts of the Irish Folklore Commission contain evidence that to have children recruited to the church carried a very high approval rating for parents in rural Ireland. As it was said, 'a priest in the family is the sign of big people'. Much the same would apply to daughters who 'took the veil'. Many had been schooled in French, music, needlework and the 'domestic skills' of housewifery and childcare, and it follows that such refinements readily equipped the daughters of respectable strong farmers to don a religious habit in order to become the schoolteachers, nurses and social care workers who formed the backbone of development in social and healthcare facilities for the masses—whether in Ireland, England or elsewhere in the world.

Not every daughter of a strong farmer was successful in achieving her ambition to become a nun. Entry registers for active communities engaged in teaching, health and social care reveal the rigour of the weeding-out process. Unsuitable would-be candidates or postulants who were not perfectly healthy in mind and body, or who were deemed too fickle to endure the strict discipline, were summarily despatched home within weeks as having 'no vocation'. The work they would be asked to do was demanding, obedience was paramount, and the training to be undergone was strict and thorough. In convent registers tart comments recorded aspirants' shortcomings: 'not a worker', 'distinctly sluggish', 'too delicate for housework', 'legs bad', 'weak eyes', 'untruthful', 'useless', 'no loss'! The girls they wanted had to be totally committed—and tough. They were the sort who nowadays volunteer for work abroad with aid agencies, who give up their free time to join women's support groups, or who counsel, teach and help care for the disadvantaged.

Evidence has shown that there could be up to twenty per cent kinship within the membership of some congregations. Encouraged by great-aunts, aunts, cousins and blood sisters who had already entered the ranks of a religious community, generation after generation of bright and gutsy girls joined their kith and kin in religious life, rolled up their sleeves and tackled social problems that not many others would touch. The majority, it must be said, subsequently spent years in lowly and obscure dedication to the work they were assigned to, but others rose high within the ranks of their chosen institutions to become formidable mother superiors who did not balk at tangling with intransigent bishops or initiating bold building projects.

Why were these daughters of the strong farmers and middle-class merchants so successful in their chosen careers? Perhaps they brought to convent life an overlooked bonus in that their family backgrounds had fostered in them an inherent business acumen and authority. It was knowledge gathered in the most traditional and basic way since childhood by listening to the talk round the table. These girls had grown up understanding the negotiating skills required by self-employed farmers for striking deals, for haggling and manoeuvring over a price. If not exactly 'street-wise' in the urban sense, it might be said that they were most certainly 'market-place aware' when it came to financial matters. They were accustomed to the supervision of farm servants and other staff and they were familiar with animal husbandry—which was useful if a convent ran a small farm, as many did. As 'daughters of the house', young Irishwomen knew how to run a middle-class household. Convent households were, in essence, exactly this and they had to conduct their affairs in a business-like manner to survive.

Research on religious communities based in England—and some of these institutions were 75 per cent reliant on Irishwomen for membership—show that a typical convent was required to balance its books and, if at all possible, to provide a small annual surplus of income over expenditure. The mother superior and her assistant, the convent bursar, were accountable for every penny spent, either to their institute's superior general or to the local bishop. Their income, for the most part, was raised from the professional work carried out, whether as

46. According to nineteenth-century Canon Law, the mother superior of a convent could 'make ordinary purchases necessary to provide shelter or clothing or which are needed for the ordinary upkeep of property. She may [perform] acts of ordinary administration…enter into contracts of buying and selling…gifts, loans, rents and all other acts of a similar nature'. (*The Catholic Directory Advertiser, 1897*)

teachers, nurses or as administrators of health and welfare institutions. A two-tier scale of fees was usually in operation, by which a proportion of payments made by the wealthy for educational, nursing, hospital or institutional care would be set aside to subsidise poor schools, gratuitous nursing services and care of the elderly, and so on. Income was also generated from money brought in to communities as dowries by the girls who were accepted. Dowries might range from as much as £1,000 to as little as £5, or even nothing at all. It is not always understood that the amount of dowry varied considerably from community to community and depended sometimes on whether the structure of the religious congregation involved class differences between choir nuns and lay sisters. Many did not employ a rule that required formal divisions. On average, a dowry was roughly commensurate with the sum expected as a marriage dowry—which in mid-nineteenth-century rural Ireland might be around £300. Such funds were invested and not touched during the lifetime of each community member.

Convents sometime received subscriptions, donations and gifts of property, or endowments from benefactors, especially from new converts to Catholicism, or from the clergy. They were always well supported by laywomen, who may have felt a particular empathy with the sisters and their work. Such funds were usually carefully invested to provide interest or collateral for borrowings. Convents took out loans and mortgages in just the same way as any other business. They could, and did, negotiate bank overdrafts. They held portfolios of shares and other financial investment packages. Legal and financial documents would be signed by the mother superior, sometimes together with her assistant or the convent bursar. A community's outgoings should be thought of in terms of an ordinary household's expenses for food, heat, light, rent and rates, insurance and so on. Added to this would be the costs of running the schools, the hospitals and the other services. School supplies had to be purchased and a wage bill covered if lay staff members were employed. Having taken vows of poverty, the sisters themselves received no personal payment for their work. The wages paid by government agencies to a religious community for professional services would be subsumed into the general income of the congregation.

Their work was costly. In the administration of hospitals, clusters of schools or asylum-type institutions, a convent community could expect to have several hundred or so extra people who needed to be provided with sustenance: patients, inmates, schoolchildren—those who through age, or homelessness or other disability were incapable of helping themselves in some way. All required food, shelter, heat, light and so on. All such convent–based activities were required to be financially viable.

It is not always realised that convent accounts were subject to annual audits, often conducted by outside accountants. Before charitable status was introduced, the religious institutions had to pay income tax and other charges. Many expanding congregations acquired large, old and sometimes unsuitable buildings in need of expensive refurbishment. Completely new premises were often built and mother superiors took personal responsibility for the supervision of construction work. They had direct dealings with surveyors, architects and building tradesmen, plumbers, carpenters, painters and decorators. Contracts were negotiated, surveyors consulted, reports and quotations drawn up, and the work finally supervised—all dealt with by the sisters as a matter of course. A letter in one archive, written by the institution's mother general, pays tribute to a convent superior whom she had entrusted with a large building programme in 1891: 'Sister Catherine of Sienna has spared herself no trouble or fatigue. She has really done the office of Clerk of the Works and I am sure must have saved thus more than £100. There would have been many mistakes without her supervision'. One hundred pounds was a considerable sum of money in those days.

By the turn of the century, some of the larger religious congregations' purchasing power was formidable and the business they conducted with local traders of substantial value. Examination of the advertising section of nineteenth- and twentieth-century Catholic Directories reveals these journals to be replete with building suppliers and wholesalers, offering plumbing and heating systems, laundry machinery, desks and school supplies of every description, in addition to day-to-day catering requirements. It was a lucrative market and one jealously guarded. However, astute reverend mothers were slow to bend to threats or persuasion from supposedly supportive Catholic tradespeople. When faced with threats of being reported to the bishop for using a non-Catholic builder and architect in Sheffield, one community merely referred the matter to their lawyer and carried on with their plans regardless. The convent archives do not record whether or not they followed the further advice of their legal team who, on hearing that the protesting traders had been led by a local Catholic bank manager, suggested that the sisters might show their disapproval of his meddling in their affairs by removing their account from his branch.

On a day–to-day basis, evidence suggests that small individual convents conducted their household expenditure with the same thrifty management as was required of any ordinary Victorian middle-class home. Good value and savings were sought in the purchase of all necessities. In the 1880s a community of sisters in Birmingham—three-quarters of whom were either Irish or from the Irish diaspora—conducted regular business with a London-based co-operative firm for delivery of groceries at discount prices. The convent bursar monitored the quality and exactitude of their supplies by carefully checking the entries in their passbook. When a charge of 4d for coffee was found to be in error, it was later carefully itemised as a credited refund. Truly an example of compliance with the Victorian moral axiom 'If you mind the pennies, the pounds will look after themselves'!

Nineteenth-century convents, having risen to become powerful and influential institutions, began their slow decline in the final quarter of the last century. Other agencies had taken on their social responsibilities in the fields of education, health and caring work and the need for their input had passed. Moreover, the well of unemployable young rural Irishwomen had dried up. It may be seen now that convent life in the last two centuries had created an unprecedented dynamic which, despite inherent failings and faults, endeavoured bravely to respond to the needs of the time. The contribution made by the thousands of Irishwomen who left Ireland to become nuns has been of inestimable merit. While often hidden and unacknowledged, the power and influence they wielded are undeniable and their work, when weighed up against the vacuum that had previously existed in education, health and social care, was staggeringly worthwhile.

Chapter 12

Swapping Canada for Ireland:
the Fenian invasion of 1866

David A. Wilson

They slipped across the Niagara River from Buffalo to Fort Erie before dawn on 1 June 1866—some 600 Irish veterans of the American Civil War, under the command of Monaghan-born John O'Neill. 300 miles to the east, in New York and Vermont, more were gathering on the Canadian border. In their dispatches, they described themselves as the 'Right wing IRA'. Their mission? To strike a blow at the British Empire, to avenge the oppression of their country, and to trigger a chain of events that would culminate in the liberation of Ireland. The Great Famine had produced massive migration from Ireland to the United States; the American Civil War had transformed thousands of those immigrants into soldiers; and the Irish Republican Brotherhood (IRB), or Fenians, was seizing the opportunity to turn them against British power. Getting them across the Atlantic to start an Irish revolution was out of the question, but Canada appeared wide open for invasion.

If the Fenians could take Canada, all seemed possible. The country could become a base from which to disrupt transatlantic British commerce, or become a bargaining chip in negotiations to secure an independent Ireland. And if this seemed too far-fetched—as indeed it was—another, more plausible, scenario presented itself. By invading Canada from the United States, by defeating the forces of the Crown and by establishing a presence on British American soil, the Fenians could precipitate an Anglo-American war. Relations between Britain and the United States had deteriorated during the Civil War (the UK had been sympathetic to the South), and Secretary of State William Seward had supposedly let it be known that he would 'recognise accomplished facts' if the invasion was successful. In addition, a Fenian victory in Canada would inspire the revolutionary movement back home at the very moment when British troops were being pulled towards British North America. And judging by the response of moderate nationalists in Ireland to news of the invasion, this was not far off the mark. Upon learning that O'Neill's men had defeated the Canadian militia at the Battle of Ridgeway in the Niagara peninsula, *The Nation* exulted that 'for the first time in well-nigh 70 years the red flag of England has gone down before the Irish green'; such news, it added, 'fills our people with tumultuous emotions impossible to describe, impossible to conceal'. If this was how moderate nationalists reacted, the feelings of Irish Fenians must have been off the scale. England's difficulty would become Ireland's opportunity, and Ireland would be freed on the plains of Canada. That, at any rate, was the theory.

The Fenian strategy was riddled with miscalculations, however. The US government was more interested in winning the Irish Catholic vote than in risking war with Britain, and its officials on the ground quickly moved to prevent Fenian reinforcements from crossing into Canada. Meanwhile, in New York and Vermont, the number of Fenians at the border fell far short of the leaders' expectations, and their tentative foray into Canada was easily repulsed. Even if more of them had arrived, it would have made little difference. The Fenian leaders believed that French Canadians, as fellow victims of British imperialism, would remain neutral, and that Irish-Canadian Catholics would refuse to fight against their fellow countrymen; it would then be relatively easy to isolate British military garrisons, and to force Canadian Orangemen to 'surrender in detail' or be 'cut to pieces by our troops'. All these assumptions proved false; most Canadians, English-speaking and French-speaking alike, regarded the Fenians as invaders rather than liberators.

Most, but not all. There is a secret history of the Fenian invasion attempts that has escaped the attention of many Canadian historians and commentators, who have traditionally regarded Fenianism solely as an external threat, and have focused their attention on the connection between the Fenian raids of 1866 and the establishment of the Canadian Confederation the following year. The standard Canadian take on the Fenians runs as follows: they were a bunch of embittered revolutionaries who came up with a bizarre and hare-brained scheme to free Ireland by invading the inoffensive people of Canada; their military operations turned out to be a farce (the phrase 'comic opera' recurs repeatedly in the historiography); and the consequences of their actions were the very reverse of their intentions, since their invasion actually strengthened Canadian nationalism and the cause of confederation rather than turning the country into a republic.

Such a view not only underestimates the strength of purpose of American Fenianism, and forgets that Canadian confederation was a done deal before the invasion, but also misses the most interesting part of the story—the Fenian movement in Canada itself, and its role in these events. It is the story of Irish-Canadian revolutionaries who plotted to bring down the Canadian state, and of the government's reaction to the threat within. Although most Irish Catholics in Canada did not support the Fenian invasion, a militant minority was prepared to support the strategy by destroying telegraph and railway communications, burning down government and financial buildings, taking Canadian politicians hostage, suborning Irish soldiers in British regiments, spiking artillery guns

47. An April 1907 land grant certificate from the province of Ontario to
Henry Pulty Timmerman, a veteran of the Fenian invasion of 1870.
(National Museum of Ireland)

48. Thomas D'Arcy McGee (left) – the former Young Ireland revolutionary
    became Canada's leading opponent of Fenianism. He was assassinated by a
    Fenian bullet on 7 April 1868. A reward poster for the apprehension of the
    assassin (right). (Multitext)

and infiltrating the Canadian militia. To coordinate their activities, the Fenian
'general' Tom Sweeny established his own 'secret service corps in Canada'.
Secrecy and deception were the order of the day. Canadian Fenians worked
through and controlled front organisations such as the Hibernian Benevolent

Society in Toronto and the St Patrick's Society in Montreal; they effectively took over many of the country's St Patrick's Day parades; and they feigned loyalty while planning revolution.

Francis Bernard McNamee, the man who started the Fenian movement in Montreal (and who was later suspected of being a government spy), was a case in point. In public, he proclaimed his loyalty to the queen and called for an Irish militia company to defend Canada against the Fenians. In private, he wrote that the real purpose of an Irish militia company would be to assist the Fenian invasion, adding for good measure that if the government denied his request he would raise the cry of anti-Irish Catholic discrimination and bring more of his aggrieved countrymen into the Fenian Brotherhood.

Viewing these developments with increasing alarm was Thomas D'Arcy McGee, the former Young Ireland revolutionary who had become Canada's leading opponent of Fenianism, and who was accordingly reviled by the Fenians as the archetypal apostate. 'Canada and British America', he wrote, 'have never known an enemy so subtle, so irrational, so hard to trace, and, therefore, so difficult to combat.' McGee and his fellow cabinet ministers were faced with a very real problem: how could they defeat a revolutionary minority inside an ethno-religious group without alienating the moderate majority within that group? The task was made even harder by the fact that many Irish-Canadian Catholics were ambivalent about Fenianism. Beyond a hard core of *circa* 3,000 sworn Fenians (out of an Irish Catholic population of *circa* 250,000) there was a Fenian subculture embracing many Irish labourers, artisans and small manufacturers in urban areas, along with pockets of farmers in Irish Catholic rural neighbourhoods. Some had brought their Fenian sympathies with them from Ireland; others were radicalised by local Orange and Green conflicts in Canada. Within this subculture, there were those who supported revolution in Ireland but not in Canada, and those who supported the end of a separate Irish republic but rejected the means of physical force. And moving further outwards, many constitutional nationalists had ambivalent feelings about the Fenians, believing that their hearts were in the right place even if their actions were misguided.

For his part, McGee adopted a confrontational approach, which was designed to cut through the ambivalence and to isolate and marginalise the Fenians through a strategy of polarisation. Although McGee certainly succeeded in rallying conservative Irish-Canadian Catholics against the Fenians, his overall strategy did not work, and may even have backfired. It certainly had a high personal cost; he received numerous Fenian death threats, culminating in his assassination on an Ottawa street in 1868.

While McGee urged his compatriots to draw a *cordon sanitaire* around the Fenians, the government stepped up its security measures to counter the internal and external Fenian threat. A Canadian secret police service had already been established in early 1865 in reaction to the activities of Fenians on the

49. A wanted poster for John McCafferty, a former captain in the Confederate cavalry and participant in the 1866 Fenian invasion of Canada. According to the London Metropolitan Police gazette 'special memorandum' he was still active eighteen years later in the dynamite campaign in Britain. (National Museum of Ireland)

Canada–US border; from the autumn it was expanded, and focused exclusively on the Fenians. Spies attempted to infiltrate the movement, with mixed results, and informers supplied the government with intelligence that varied greatly in quality; it became increasingly difficult to separate fact from fantasy.

To check the sources, the government intercepted and read cross-border mail, and sent freelance spies down to the Fenian headquarters at New York. The British consulates in New York, Buffalo, Boston and Philadelphia were also rich sources of information. There were so many shady Fenian informers paying nocturnal visits to the British consul in New York, the Nova Scotia-born Edward Archibald, that his daughter began to fear for his life. Even the Dublin Metropolitan Police got in on the act, sending their own spy to New York. He used the codename D. Thomas—a rather risky choice since his real name was Thomas Doyle.

Nevertheless, the Canadian authorities were taken completely by surprise when the Fenians invaded from Buffalo in May–June 1866. In response, the government suspended habeas corpus for one year, and fortified the parliamentary and administrative buildings in Ottawa, to protect them against 'the sudden introduction of explosive preparations'. As long as the threat remained, the suspension of habeas corpus continued; it was renewed in November 1867, amid concerns about another invasion, and it was suspended again in the spring and summer of 1868, in the aftermath of McGee's assassination.

Despite—or because of—complaints from Orangemen that it was being too soft, and from radical Irish nationalists that it was being too hard, the government generally managed to steer a middle course between complacency and alarmism. In the process, it helped to check an anti-Irish Catholic backlash that would only have made the situation worse, and also managed to retain much of its existing Irish Catholic support. Some twenty-five people were arrested under the suspension of habeas corpus, and most of them would be released within six months, on the grounds that Fenianism was dead in the United States and had been stamped out in Canada.

The belief was wrong; the Fenian movement in Canada had indeed been damaged by the assassination and the arrests, but it had not been comprehensively defeated, and its most militant members continued to prepare for the next American invasion, which eventually occurred in the summer of 1870 with the Battle of Eccles Hill. But where Ridgeway could be presented as a Fenian victory of sorts, the Battle of Eccles Hill was a humiliating failure. This time the Canadian authorities were fully informed and fully prepared; they decided to let the invasion go ahead so that they could deliver a crushing blow to the Fenians and discredit the whole idea of liberating Ireland by way of Canada. It worked; confronted with superior military force, the Fenians sensibly turned back to the United States as fast as their feet would carry them.

Henceforth, Irish-Canadian nationalism, in both its revolutionary and constitutional forms, would be focused directly on Ireland.

Chapter 13

A training school for rebels: Fenians in the French Foreign Legion

James McConnell and Máirtín Ó Catháin

In 1920, six years before Hollywood made the film *Beau Geste*, Bray and Arklow in County Wicklow doubled for North Africa in another, less famous silent film about the French Foreign Legion made by the Celtic Cinema Company, entitled *Rosaleen Dhu*. Based on a story by John Denvir, the film tells the romantic tale of an exiled Fenian who joins the Legion and later marries an Algerian woman, only to discover that she is the heiress to a large Irish estate. Such escapism was probably welcome in 1920 as the War of Independence entered its bloodiest phase, but, in the best tradition of film-making, the tale was, in fact, 'based on a true story'. During the nineteenth century a considerable number of Irishmen served in the *Légion Etrangère*, and a number of them were indeed members of the IRB.

Irish service in the armies of France dated back to the 'Wild Geese' of the seventeenth and eighteenth centuries and officially ended in 1792, when the 'Irish Brigade' was disbanded. The French Foreign Legion was created 40 years later, in 1831, as a unit for foreign volunteers, primarily to protect and extend France's overseas empire. Irishmen served with the Legion almost from the start. One of Thomas Moore's sons died serving in North Africa in 1846, while a Captain Patrick Brangan served with the Legion in the 1850s. Most famously, Marshal MacMahon of France, the descendant of County Limerick 'Wild Geese', commanded the Legion during the 1840s and was later responsible for the suppression of the Paris Commune in 1871.

In 1851, seven years before the IRB was established, one of its founders, Thomas Clarke Luby, set out for France intent on joining the Foreign Legion in order to learn infantry tactics. The Legion had temporarily suspended recruitment at the time, however, and so his ambition was frustrated. This is the first known instance of Irish separatists identifying the Legion as a training school for rebels, though the idea of going abroad to acquire military experience was then current. The Cork Fenian J. F. X. O'Brien took part in William Walker's 1855 filibuster in Nicaragua for much the same purpose.

An angst-ridden father's chiding of his rebellious son persuaded John Devoy 'to run away and join the Zouaves'. (Initially recruited solely from the Zouaoua, a tribe of North African Berbers, the flamboyantly dressed Zouaves evolved into an elite French force.) The 18-year-old Fenian had already secured the requisite letters of introduction and successfully resisted the appeals of his chief, James Stephens, to join the American military instead. The Paris correspondent of the *Irishman*, J. P. Leonard, took the young Devoy and his request to be a Zouave to the French Ministry of War, where it was confirmed to him that as a foreigner he was only able to join the French Foreign Legion. Devoy's service with the Legion, however, was short and far from action-packed for one seeking combat training and experience. After reading reports of the escalating crisis in the United States and of the funeral of Terence Bellew MacManus in Dublin, he decided to return to Ireland. He withdrew from the Legion officially on 5 March 1862, having served less than a year but with enough French to impress Stephens and the wherewithal to train others in the rudiments of soldiering.

James J. O'Kelly joined the IRB in 1861, and after moving to London he quickly became leader of the city's Fenians. He fell out with James Stephens, however, and in 1864 resolved to join the Legion. O'Kelly and Devoy had been boyhood friends, and the latter's example doubtless influenced him. Devoy actually warned him of the hardships of Algerian service and of the likelihood that the Legion would be deployed to support the French-sponsored Emperor Maximillian against the Mexican republic. Notwithstanding Devoy's republican scruples, O'Kelly resolved to enlist. Indeed, his service in North Africa suggests that he was able to reconcile himself to French colonialism. According to Tim Healy, O'Kelly later recounted the story of how he had once 'debated within himself, when placed as a sentry over Moorish prisoners, whether he would shoot them if they tried to escape, but resolved that if they did he would act as a Frenchman'.

As Devoy predicted, the Legion was sent to Mexico. O'Kelly apparently fought in several battles, though he always remained tight-lipped about his Mexican service. Thirty years later he claimed that after the 'disastrous battle of Mier' he and other stragglers had made their way to New Orleans. In fact, it seems that the discipline of the 1st and 2nd Battalions of the *Légion Etrangère* snapped as the French intervention faltered during 1866 and that, after looting the deserted town, eighty-nine Legionnaires deserted. Devoy certainly claimed that when O'Kelly was informed about the planned rising in Ireland he 'took the first chance of deserting', eventually making his way to New York.

In the aftermath of the unsuccessful rising of 1867, O'Kelly was involved in rebuilding the IRB in Ireland and supporting early Fenian attempts to cooperate with Isaac Butt's emerging Home Rule movement. The outbreak of the Franco-Prussian War in 1870, however, saw O'Kelly return to the French

50. Six years before Hollywood made *Beau Geste* (1926), Bray and Arklow
doubled for North Africa in the Celtic Cinema Company's *Rosaleen Dhu*,
a romantic tale of an exiled Fenian who joins the French Foreign Legion.

colours. Having satisfactorily accounted for his disappearance four years earlier, O'Kelly was commissioned colonel and undertook to recruit a new 'Irish Brigade' for the French army. Setting up his base in Liverpool, he was in the process of recruiting Irishmen when Paris surrendered. O'Kelly was by no means the only Fenian to fight for France against Prussia, however.

The same odd conglomeration behind the pre-Fenian campaigns of the MacMahon Sword presentation (in recognition of his command of the victorious French campaign in northern Italy in 1859), the Irish Papal Brigade and the National Petition (a plebiscite on Irish self-determination in 1860) re-emerged in the post-Fenian hiatus of 1870; it sponsored the idea of an Irish ambulance unit in support of the French in the opening days of the Franco-Prussian war. The idea of the ambulance was partly the result of the previous efforts to raise the Irish Papal Brigade in the service of Rome against the French and Italians. Recruitment was restricted by the threatened enforcement of the Foreign Enlistment Act of 1819. The ambulance would circumvent the legislation, draw philanthropic support and offer useful practical aid to the French while avoiding the taint of treasonable ulterior motives. A subsequent gathering of suitably respectable, mildly nationalist Francophile medics, bandage-dressers and stretcher-bearers—including, perhaps unsurprisingly,

51. *Bataille de Fontenoy, 11 Mai 1745* by Horace Vernet – the Irish Brigade turned the battle in France's favour, part of a long tradition of Irish military for France. (Réunion de Musée Nationaux)

52. Thomas Clarke Luby – in 1851, seven years before the IRB was established, he set out for France intent on joining the Foreign Legion in order to learn infantry tactics. (Multitext)

a fair quota of Fenians—met in the autumn of 1870 in Dublin to prepare for dispatch to Le Havre. At 400-strong, for the staffing of four ambulances, the unit was implausibly large but provided adequate cover for the organisation of a breakaway volunteer corps of soldiers. They were commanded by a scion of the Waters Kirwan family of Galway who was an ex-British Army officer and a keen sympathiser of the Fenians. He was later active in Home Rule circles before emigrating to Canada, where he achieved high rank in the army and helped stifle Louis Riel's 1885 Northwest rebellion. Captain Martin Waters Kirwan took command of a 100-strong segment of the 'ambulance' once in France, formed into a company and attached to the 2nd *Regiment Étranger* (the Legion at this time having dwindled to only a couple of regiments). Kirwan's staff was complemented by a medic released by the ambulance, Dr Macken, the Legion veteran Frank McAlevy and the former Fenians, Terence Byrne and Martin Carey.

The ambivalence, incompetence and privation of life in the *Regiment Étranger* during the winter of 1870-71 did not entirely destroy the morale of the Irish company under Kirwan. The support of provincial dignitaries and the wonderment of the rural peasantry, combined with the action of engagements with Prussian troops and examples made by the French, such as the execution of a Polish soldier for selling some of his kit, ensured that mutinous talk was kept to a minimum. The Irish proved capable enough, despite hunger, dysentery and frostbite, and fought well with surprisingly few casualties at Montbelliard, covering thereafter the retreat to Besançon until the armistice in February 1871. The ambulance under a Dr Baxter remained in Le Havre after the departure of Kirwan's company in October 1870, but little else is known of their subsequent activities, though it contained some august names such as Thomas More Madden, the famous Irish gynaecologist son of R. R. Madden, and Charles William McCarthy, who became a renowned surgeon in Australia in later years. The majority of Kirwan's men returned to Ireland at the cessation of hostilities, wary of being accused of being mercenaries, and only one individual, Lieutenant B. Cotter, chose to return with the Regiment to Algeria.

James Stephens, forever trying to re-ingratiate himself into Fenian circles since his fall from grace in the mid-1860s, had also responded to pressure from his supporters in Ireland to form an Irish unit in support of the French at the outbreak of the war. This, however, appears to have had little tangible effect other than a mooted drawing together of the divided Fenian movement. Instead, Stephens travelled to Paris alone and attempted to engage the embattled government of the French Republic.

Besides Kirwan's outfit, there was one other group of Irishmen, some of them Fenians, who took part in the Franco-Prussian conflict in the ranks of the French Foreign Legion. This group appears to have been organised by some of the London Irish, possibly prompted by the local IRB. By the time Kirwan's volunteers had arrived, most of this group had already returned to England under a cloud owing to their 'ingenuity' in supplementing meagre

53. John Devoy (left) as a prisoner in 1866. This was six years before the chiding of an angst-ridden father persuaded the then 18-year-old to run away and join the Zouaves
54. The Zouaves were a flamboyantly dressed elite French force, but as a foreigner Devoy was only able to join the French Foreign Legion. (National Museum of Ireland)

French military rations. Bernard Molloy, James Lysaght Finigan and Edmund O'Donovan were among the forty or so who remained with the Legion and who served until the war ended. Although not known to have been a Fenian, Molloy had already served with the Papal Zouaves (attaining the rank of captain) when he joined the Legion.

Although Finigan was a middle-class, Liverpool-Irish tea merchant, he had Fenian connections and military ambitions. He had formerly volunteered for the Papal Zouaves and with the outbreak of war enlisted at Tours with the Legion, where he quickly recognised O'Donovan, who was serving under an assumed name. O'Donovan was a Trinity-educated journalist, recruited into the IRB by O'Donovan Rossa. During the 1860s he was head-centre of a circle of Trinity students and was imprisoned on several occasions for his activities. Although O'Donovan doubted the wisdom of the 1867 rising, he participated and subsequently escaped to France. According to Finigan, many of the Irish Legionaries had also experienced 'troublesome times on the hillsides of Ireland' and spent time in 'British dungeons'. The Irish suffered heavy casualties during the winter campaign and were involved in the French defeat at the second battle of Orléans in December 1870. Finigan and O'Donovan were captured, with the latter being sent to Bavaria as a prisoner-of-war. Finigan later entered parliament as a Parnellite, while O'Donovan subsequently became a distinguished journalist, losing his life in 1883 covering the Sudan campaign.

The Franco-Prussian War witnessed the end of an Irish tradition of French military service that stretched back to the seventeenth century. A considerable number of those who served were Fenians, motivated by Francophile sentiment, Jacobite romanticism or a desire to acquire military training. After the defeat of the second empire of Napoleon III, Irishmen continued to serve in the Legion, though in smaller numbers. The most notable among this later group was the Corkonian Michael MacWhite, who served with the Legion in France, Greece and Turkey during the Great War and was awarded the *Croix de Guerre* three times before embarking on a 30-year-long career as an Irish diplomat. MacWhite, like his Fenian Legionnaire predecessors, fought against the Hohenzollerns. Indeed, in his dotage and after a long career as a journalist, adventurer, Fenian and Parnellite lieutenant, J. J. O'Kelly remained a strong supporter of France in 1914. In contrast, after 1900 neo-Fenians made common cause with Germany, though Roger Casement could induce only fifty-two men to join his German 'Irish Brigade', in contrast to the many thousands of Irishmen who had volunteered for French service in previous centuries.

Chapter 14

The Friends of Irish freedom: a case-study in Irish-American Nationalism, 1916-21

Michael Doorley

Historically, nationalists in Ireland have looked to their cousins in the United States for both financial assistance and diplomatic support. This support has never been a foregone conclusion, but at critical moments in Irish history, usually during times of political tension, Irish-America has taken a keen interest in Irish events. During the turmoil of the Land War, with its news of evictions and the threat of renewed famine, Irish-American organisations such as the Irish National League of America garnered much support for Parnell's political campaigns in Ireland. Subsequently, the United Irish League (UIL) also provided valuable financial support for John Redmond's Irish Parliamentary Party, especially as prospects for Irish Home Rule brightened in the years before the First World War.

The Friends of Irish Freedom (FOIF) was founded a few weeks prior to the 1916 Rising, ostensibly to promote the cause of Ireland in the United States. In their first constitution, they pledged themselves 'to encourage and assist any movement that will tend to bring about the national independence of Ireland'. Yet, as we shall see, there were also American factors behind their foundation. The evolving character of the Irish immigrant group, as well as the American political environment, heavily influenced the history of the movement, often giving rise to misunderstandings of a fundamental nature on both sides of the Atlantic.

It was another Irish-American organisation, the Clan na Gael, that played a key role in the foundation and direction of the Friends. Of the seventeen-man FOIF executive, fifteen were Clan members. Founded in 1867, the Clan was a secret revolutionary society dedicated to the cause of an Irish republic. It was involved in all kinds of activities, ranging from the rescue of Fenian prisoners in Australia to commissioning Irish engineer and ex-Christian Brother John P. Holland to build a submarine to take on the British navy. It also had well-established contacts with its counterpart in Ireland, the IRB. The Clan's role in the 1916 Rising has been well documented. Its leader, John Devoy, knew of the impending rising and no doubt wanted to have a propaganda organisation in place in America to exploit the expected news from Ireland. The FOIF was founded at the First Irish Race Convention on

55. On top of Manhattan's Waldorf-Astoria hotel in 1919 – (left to right) Harry Boland, Liam Mellows (leader of the '1916 exiles'), Diarmuid Lynch (secretary of the Friends of Irish Freedom), Dr Patrick McCartan (Irish envoy to Washington), and, sitting, John Devoy (leader of Clan na Gael). (De Valera Papers, UCD Archives. Courtesy of the UCD-OFM Partnership)

4 March 1916, at New York's Hotel Astor. The convention attracted 2,300 delegates, many of high social standing. As Devoy later proudly pointed out in his memoirs: 'At no previous Irish convention was there even one [state] supreme court judge; there were five at this, besides several other judges of lesser rank, and a large number of lawyers'.

Judge Daniel Cohalan, who helped Devoy to reunite the Clan in 1900 after the factionalism of the previous decade, became the acknowledged leader of the Friends. Cohalan, whose parents came from Ireland, typified the great social strides many Irish-Americans had made by the early twentieth century. Elected to New York's supreme court in 1911, his voluminous papers reveal a man who exercised considerable influence in American politics, especially with members of the Republican Party and with the Irish-dominated Catholic hierarchy.

As with other Irish-American organisations, both before and since, events in Ireland helped to publicise the FOIF among Irish-Americans. Irish-American opinion was outraged by the executions that followed the 1916 Rising, and the Friends capitalised on this to the utmost. The organisation did not achieve its full numerical strength until after the First World War, however. During the Anglo-Irish war, as lurid news of the Black and Tans' atrocities reached Irish-America, membership soared. By the summer of 1920 the organisation numbered 100,000 regular members and an additional 175,000 associate members. It opened the Irish National Bureau in Washington, which distributed a *Newsletter* and countless pamphlets and leaflets to thousands of prominent Americans and opinion-formers. The Friends also sought to use their numbers to put the Irish case for self-determination before the US Congress and president, though with mixed success.

One might have expected a close working relationship between the Friends and what became the main nationalist party in Ireland, Sinn Féin. Éamon de Valera believed that the Friends could be used to secure 'the great lever of American opinion' in support of Irish objectives in Ireland. Relations between the movements were dogged by tension and conflict, however. The Friends resented the dictation of Sinn Féin representatives in the United States and believed that the direction of the organisation should be in American hands. Matters came to such a head that Bishop Michael Gallagher, the president of the Friends, denounced de Valera as a 'foreign potentate'. Finally, in October 1920, in an atmosphere of mutual recrimination, Sinn Féin publicly severed its ties with the FOIF.

While personality differences between Cohalan and de Valera certainly contributed to this conflict, there was a deeper ideological conflict between the Irish-American nationalism represented by the Friends and the Irish nationalism of Sinn Féin. At this point the Catholic Irish in America had improved their social position compared to their degraded status during the era of the Great Famine. Yet despite these advances, Irish-Americans still felt discriminated against by what Devoy referred to as a pro-British Anglo-Saxon elite. It was felt that this elite not only denied Irish-Americans their rightful place in American society but also identified as much with the interests of Britain as they did with the United States. In response, Irish-Americans founded societies such as the American Irish Historical Society (1896), which emphasised their loyalty to the American nation. The Irish contribution to American colonial history and the heroic Irish contribution to America's wars became a characteristic feature of the society's publications. Cohalan joined the society in 1898 and served as a member of its executive council for nearly forty years.

Irish ethnic opposition to the perceived pro-British element in the United States also took on a political dimension and increasingly influenced the activities of the Clan in the decades before the First World War. Devoy and Cohalan feared that any close cooperation between Britain and the United

States would increase the power of the 'Anglo' elite in American society. This cooperation would be detrimental not only to the interests of Irish-America but also to America itself. In 1897, following calls for a comprehensive arbitration treaty that would settle all outstanding disputes between the United States and Britain, Devoy's wing of the Clan despatched resolutions to the president and both houses of Congress protesting against its ratification.

In the event, the Senate failed to ratify the treaty (for reasons other than Irish-American pressure). Yet the vociferous opposition of Devoy to this measure indicates the Clan's increasing identification of the interests of Irish-America with those of the United States. The founding of the *Gaelic American* in 1903 offers further evidence for this increasing American orientation to the Clan's activities. The newspaper was edited by Devoy, with Cohalan as president of its board of directors. In its first edition (19 September 1903) the paper referred to Irish-Americans as 'the sturdiest champions of American principles', but argued that 'these principles were assailed at the very fountain head by an organised movement to destroy the old American spirit and substitute for it a servile dependence on England'. The editorial warned that 'a clique of pro-British sycophants' were seeking to gain control over the direction of American foreign policy.

Again in 1912, the Clan, in alliance with other Irish-American and German-American organisations, focused its energies on defeating yet another Anglo-American arbitration treaty before the Senate. A joint petition of the United German-American and United Irish-American societies of New York was despatched to the Senate, stating that 'the propaganda carried on in favor of the Treaty is essentially pro-English and offensive to citizens of other races, who now constitute a majority of the population of the United States . . . We emphatically deny that the majority of the American people are of English race or that the portion of them who are partly of English blood are in favor of alliance with England'. In the years before the First World War, Devoy in his correspondence with Cohalan talked about the need to found an open public organisation in order to combat what he termed the pro-British conspiracy in the United States. Writing to Cohalan in November 1911, Devoy expressed anger about plans for the celebration of 'a hundred years of peace with England'. Devoy argued that leading American political figures, notably Theodore Roosevelt and William Jennings Bryan, were behind plans that advocated textbooks in schools emphasising Anglo-American friendship, 'a free commemorative bridge over the Niagara river, a great free building in New York or some other city, and the purchase of the original Washington estates in England, with a number of celebrations thrown in'. Devoy argued that battling such schemes 'gives us work for the next four years. But we must do it through a public American organisation.'

Prior to 1914, the chances of establishing an organisation dedicated to combating British influence in America seemed remote. Irish revolutionary nationalism was at a low ebb on both sides of the Atlantic, while the apparent

56. Friends of Irish Freedom Victory Drive leaflet (1919), depicting soldiers of the Irish-American 69th Regiment in action during the First World War. (American Irish Historical Society)

success of John Redmond's Irish Parliamentary Party disappointed and frustrated the Clan leadership. Events in Ireland played into the hands of the Clan, however. Redmond's declaration of support for the British war effort in 1914 alienated much of Irish-American opinion, and his popularity among Irish-Americans declined far more rapidly than it did in Ireland. In August 1915 the *Irish World*, an Irish-American newspaper that had previously supported Redmond, now argued that for Redmond to 'fritter away any part of her [Ireland's] military resources by going to England's defence would be treason of the blackest kind'. Meanwhile, the UIL, Redmond's support organisation in the United States, went into rapid decline.

In 1916 the Clan went ahead with their convention, which provided the launch pad for the FOIF, now representative of a largely united Irish-America. While speeches denouncing Redmond and advocating Irish independence were a major focus of the convention's deliberations, it is also clear from its 'declaration of principles' that the task of countering pro-British influence in the United States and ensuring continued American neutrality was a major aim of the new organisation. The declaration insisted that the United States should not enter the war as England's ally. In a pointed reference to the sinking of the *Lusitania*, mention was made of Britain's current attempts to 'shield her floating arsenals and munitions transports behind the skirts of American women and children'. In March 1916 the *Gaelic American* also declared after the convention that 'the pro-British movement is now confronted by an organised Irish race throughout the land'.

The outbreak of the Easter Rising in Dublin, a mere six weeks after the Race Convention in New York, presented the Friends with a golden opportunity to bring their message home to thousands of their fellow Americans. Mass meetings were held in areas of Irish-American settlement, condemning British atrocities in Ireland and calling for the continuation of American neutrality. The Friends also organised speaking tours for 'exiles' from Ireland such as Hannah Sheehy-Skeffington, Nora Connolly and Liam Mellows.

Nevertheless, while the FOIF was able to organise mass meetings of several thousand people, membership did not grow as one might have expected. Because of government fears that the war in Europe could provoke conflict among the different national groupings in the United States, 'Americanisation drives' were directed at those foreign-born Americans who displayed any overt identification with their country of origin. Such people were branded in the press as 'hyphen Americans'. Once the United States entered the war in April 1917, suspicion of un-Americanism and 'hyphenism' intensified. Britain was now America's ally, and attacks on British policy in Ireland could be viewed as disloyalty to the United States. As a result of this oppressive wartime atmosphere, FOIF activities were drastically scaled back and many branches ceased to function for the duration of the war. By the end of 1917 membership had fallen to just over a thousand members.

A minority within the FOIF, such as Joe McGarrity, the Clan leader in Philadelphia, disagreed with the lack of wartime activity. Cohalan, under pressure from these dissident elements, reluctantly agreed to hold a Second Race Convention in January 1918. This was a very timid affair, however, that pledged Irish-American loyalty to the war effort. Sinn Féin representatives in the United States complained bitterly about the reluctance of the Friends to speak out on Ireland's behalf. Liam Mellows told shocked delegates: 'The state of affairs at home is so desperate that you people in this country are acting like a lot of curs if you do not speak now'. Meanwhile, Hannah Sheehy-Skeffington in a letter to Peter Golden in early 1918 also noted the reluctance of Irish-Americans to become involved in any activities that might be construed as unpatriotic: 'The Irish (mainly comfortable, elderly gentlemen) come and talk about old times and the days of the Kerry dances and so forth, but the moment I talk about 1918 and what could be done *now* they close up!'

Such Irish-American reticence can also be explained by reference to traditional Irish-American support for the United States in time of war. On the eve of American entry into the war, the Clan issued a circular that read: 'We will remain loyal and will yield to none in the devotion to the flag, whether the United States goes to war or remains at peace'. The mainly Irish-American 69th regiment under 'Wild Bill' Donovan was one of the first American units

57. Judge Daniel Cohalan—
    personality differences
    between him and Dev
    masked a deeper ideological
    conflict between the Irish-
    American nationalism
    represented by the Friends
    and the Irish nationalism of
    Sinn Féin (Image courtesy
    United States Library of
    Congress)

to go to the European front, and indeed featured in FOIF publicity material for an 'Irish Victory Fund' after the war.

The FOIF expanded dramatically once the shadow of war had passed. A Third Race Convention was held in Philadelphia in February 1919 with over 5,000 delegates. Diarmuid Lynch, national secretary of the Friends, estimated that over thirty Catholic bishops attended, including the influential Cardinal Gibbons of Baltimore. The tumultuous events in Ireland were also exploited to the full to expand membership. The Friends welcomed the triumph of Sinn Féin at the 1918 election in Ireland and the defeat of the despised Home Rule party of John Redmond. Indeed, Éamon de Valera, who had been born in New York, was publicly welcomed as an American hero during his visit in 1919. Yet, behind the scenes, numerous disagreements surfaced between the Friends and Sinn Féin. As early as April 1919, Devoy pointed out in a letter to Harry Boland: 'Every man who comes here from Ireland not alone misunderstands America, but is filled with preconceived notions that are wholly without foundation, as

58. Joseph McGarrity with his wife and nine children in 1919. Once the United States entered the war in April 1917, FOIF activities were drastically scaled back and many branches ceased to function for the duration of the war. A minority within the organisation, such as McGarrity, Clan na Gael leader in Philadelphia, disagreed with the lack of wartime activity. (De Valera Papers, UCD Archives. Courtesy of the UCD-OFM Partnership)

well as a belief that he knows America better than those who have spent most of their lives in the country or were born in it'.

The Friends wanted to link Irish national demands to President Wilson's peace plan for national self-determination for the oppressed peoples of Europe. Sinn Féin representatives believed, however, that such calls could be construed in Ireland as something less than the Irish Republic that the men of 1916 had died for. In June 1920 Cohalan, drawing on his influential political contacts, had persuaded the Republican Party at its Chicago convention to include Irish self-determination in their election platform. Much to the consternation of the Friends, however, de Valera's insistence on a resolution calling for the recognition of the Irish Republic led to the abandonment of Cohalan's proposal. In a pointed reference to de Valera's appearance at the Chicago convention, complete with marching bands and torchlight parades, in June 1920 the FOIF *Newsletter* condemned the 'brass band' dictatorial methods of those who refused to be guided, advised or led by 'American brains'.

The Friends' use of the Irish Victory Fund in their vociferous campaign against the League of Nations also became a major source of contention. Sinn Féin had not yet formulated a policy on the League, and felt in any case that the money collected should be sent to Ireland. The FOIF's opposition to the League, however, was consistent with the Clan's pre-war campaign to prevent an English alliance with the United States. Both Cohalan and Devoy saw Wilson's idea of a League of Nations as a deadly threat to American sovereignty and yet another attempt to entangle the United States in an alliance for the protection of the British Empire. This campaign was perfectly compatible with the goal of combating the pro-British element in the United States and would also help Ireland, since Devoy believed that the League would safeguard the integrity of the United Kingdom and prevent the emergence of an independent Ireland. As Devoy pointed out to a bemused Patrick McCartan, Sinn Féin's representative in the United States, in April 1919: 'Cohalan is making a superb fight against it, you ignore it and want the fight against it dropped. Judged by this acid test, which of you is the better friend of the Irish Republic?'

By September 1920, after de Valera's proposals to reform the FOIF had been roundly defeated, an open split had become inevitable. The majority of senior officers remained with Cohalan, though this was not true of rank-and-file members. By 1921 the FOIF had fallen to 20,000 members. Nevertheless, the movement still functioned. Interestingly, the Friends took the side of the Free State during the Civil War, blaming de Valera for the conflict. A prominent member of the Friends, Bishop William Turner of Buffalo, described de Valera as the 'Pancho Villa of Ireland', a reference to the Mexican revolutionary who had raided the United States in 1916. Meanwhile, Devoy, writing in the *Gaelic American* on 2 September 1922, described de Valera as 'a monster who must be punished for his crimes. Eliminate him and the trouble will soon end.'

The Friends welcomed the triumph of the pro-Treaty side in the Irish Civil War. In 1923 Cohalan, accompanied by Diarmuid Lynch, national secretary of the FOIF, visited Ireland and was warmly welcomed by Free State leaders. John Devoy was also awarded an official welcome on his visit to Ireland in 1924. The Friends were still incensed, however, at the Free State's application for League of Nations membership. In May 1923, the FOIF reprinted and distributed an article from the *Gaelic American* published on 28 April 1923 entitled 'The Free State makes bad blunder in applying for League membership'. The article claimed that Ireland would achieve nothing by being in the League and would only serve as 'bait' to draw the United States in. The Friends went on to argue that such a move would 'deprive it of the sympathy and support of millions of Americans of Irish blood'.

The credibility of the Friends as the voice of Irish-America would soon be open to question, however. The ending of the Anglo-Irish War and Irish-American horror at the civil war that followed had a devastating impact on the movement, as it did on other Irish-American organisations. As Irish-Americans lost interest in Ireland, support dwindled. By 1928 membership had fallen to only 654. In 1935 the FOIF was finally wound up, and its records were transferred to the American Irish Historical Society.

The development of the FOIF illustrates the impact of the changing character of the Irish immigrant group in America and the American political situation on Irish-American nationalism. Irish-Americans took pride in their American identity and their contribution to the American nation, and this sense of American identity also coloured the Irish-American nationalism of the FOIF. Given the increasing tensions between Sinn Féin and the FOIF, especially over the dispersal of the Victory Fund, a public rupture between both bodies was inevitable. Predictably, when this open breach did take place in November 1920, each side blamed the other for the split. Yet in reality neither side was to blame. The nationalist ideology of each movement was shaped by the social and political milieu in which it operated. Each felt fully justified in its actions and neither side quite understood the other.

Chapter 15

The Orange Order in Africa

Rachel Naylor

It is quite well known that the Orange Order is found outside Ireland and Britain in areas with diaspora and colonial or Commonwealth connections, such as Canada, New Zealand and Australia. Its presence on the African continent is less commonly appreciated. Orangeism had a long history in South Africa, developing in the early nineteenth century and peaking at some twenty-six lodges before disappearing in the 1960s. However, Orangeism in West Africa, with origins in the early twentieth century, is still alive.

The earliest Orange lodges in West Africa were established in Lagos, Nigeria, prior to the First World War, possibly by missionaries or, more likely, by Orangemen within the British military stationed there. The lodges were soon Africanised but these also died out in the 1960s. Some accounts suggest that this occurred in a period of clampdown on 'secret societies' by the military government or that the lodges evolved into institutions that were not recognisably 'Orange'. In West Africa today Orange lodges, African in membership, are currently found in Togo and in Ghana.

It may seem surprising that Orangeism is represented in Togo. A German colony prior to the First World War, two-thirds of its land area (including Lomé, the capital and home of Togolese Orangeism) was afterwards administered as a League of Nations mandate by France. French Togoland went on to gain its independence as Togo in 1960 and has maintained close ties with Paris and other nations in the francophone world ever since.

Although there were no strong direct colonial connections with Britain, German Togoland was briefly occupied by the British during the First World War and for two years afterwards, during which the first lodge was founded. This interlude may have provided fertile space for the Togolese Order's early development. What is more, a detailed investigation of the social milieu in which Orangeism arose in Togo reveals further connections with the British Isles. The founder of Orangeism in Togo, John A. Atayi, first learned about Orangeism from British newspapers and wrote to the Grand Lodge in England to enquire about how to set up a lodge. Atayi was a member of a well-educated, Christian, English-speaking and Anglophile class involved in overseas trade, including with British companies, and was proactive about making international connections and participating in many aspects of bourgeois British culture, from debating and literary societies to fraternities. This class tended to send their children to school in the Gold Coast (the colonial name for the southern part of Ghana) and even within the British Isles. The only surviving lodge minute book that I have come across from the period (from Atakpamé) is written entirely in English. Atayi developed the first Togo lodge after receiving his initiation in Lagos, having been directed there by the Grand Lodge of England.

What, then, might have been the attraction of Orangeism to early Togolese members, aside from its association with British society and culture? Apart from the religious elements of Orangeism, which are likely to have proved attractive to Togolese members of Protestant mission churches, economic and political advantages may have been foreseen in membership. As well as providing a local network for mutual support, international fraternal links may have been seen as a route to improving or cementing overseas trading relationships. There is certainly a well-documented attempt by the Togolese brethren to draw on these links to achieve political aspirations. In the inter-war period, when the League of Nations considered the fate of Togo, Togolese Orangemen appealed to the Grand Lodge in England to exert pressure on the secretary of state for the colonies. They wanted him to persuade the League to make Togo a British mandate.

When most of Togo became a French mandate, the organisation seemed to go into decline. There are reports that Orange property was moved the relatively short distance to Keta (under British jurisdiction) for safekeeping. In the post-colonial period, however, Orangeism was revived in conjunction with the reawakening of Ghanaian Orangeism. At its height, Togo boasted some twelve lodges in various towns. Some conducted business in English, others in French, and some, particularly the very active women's lodges, in Ewe, an important local language. Translation into Ewe undoubtedly meant an element of local 'appropriation' as Orange ritual became interpreted through local idiom and cosmology.

Togo Orange members gained their own Grand Lodge in 1985 (a separate West African Grand Lodge had existed since 1976), which not only sent representatives to the Imperial Grand Council of the World, but also provided the first African Imperial President of this over-arching Orange body in the person of Emmanuel A. Essien in 1994.

As a former British colony, which gained its independence in 1957, the existence of Orangeism in Ghana is less surprising. But here too Orangeism developed on an African initiative. R. Sharlley, a Cape Coast Post Office worker, came across Orange literature as Atayi had done and also made enquiries to the Grand Lodge in England, which put him in touch with the Order in Togo. Sharlley went on to found the first Ghanaian lodge in 1918 in his native Keta, a once-flourishing port with strong African family connections

59. Banner of the Grand Orange Lodge of Ghana on a march in the late 1990s.

with neighbouring Lomé. Again, early members seem to have been drawn from the literate Christian class of Africans, many of whom would have worked in connection with the great trading houses in the town and had family connections along the coast with Lomé. In the first Keta lodge, 'Pride of Keta', which has maintained good records, there is recorded only one non-African member since its foundation.

Orangeism in Ghana also seems to have gone through periods of growth and decline. The original enthusiasm and rapid development of lodges seems to have been in abeyance by the 1930s as members involved in the original impetus probably declined in vigour. The Depression may also have had an impact. Renewal came in the post-Second World War period, however, in the charismatic person of Revd F. K. Fiawoo of the African Methodist Episcopal Zion church. A writer, playwright and educationalist, Fiawoo is said to have 'dramatised' Orange ritual, making it more accessible to Ghanaians in terms of their understanding of it through more local idioms (further evidence of 'local' appropriation). Whilst Ghanaian Orangeism is very recognisably 'Orange' in terms of dress, activities, organisation and philosophy, it is Fiawoo's contribution to the accessibility of ritual, as well as his charismatic leadership, that is regarded as explaining its dramatic rise in popularity amongst Ghanaians after independence.

Orangeism in Ghana then went from strength to strength. A much larger country than Togo, lodges were later formed in Accra, the capital, and Tema, a significant city, and began to include more members who were non-Ewe speakers (in particular, people who would claim a Ga ethnic origin). Women's lodges and junior lodges were also formed, and at its peak in the late 1970s there were over 1000 members.

There have been periods of contraction since then. Ghana's economy, fairly buoyant at independence, declined owing to periods of political mismanagement and external factors such as the 1970s oil shocks and the fall in world prices of significant Ghanaian export commodities, particularly cocoa. Structural adjustment, largely imposed by international financial institutions in the 1980s, was supposed to address this but in turn had negative effects for most ordinary Ghanaians, struggling to make ends meet. A general decline in many forms of associational life, including Orangeism, is attributed to economic woes.

Economic difficulties also brought about political problems. A series of civilian and military governments pre-dated the 1979 and 1981 coups led by Flight Lieutenant Jerry Rawlings. His post-1981 regime sought to suppress 'lodges'

60. Togbi Subo II (front), Superintendent of Juniors of the Grand Lodge of Ghana and Ewe chief, with juniors from two of Ghana's juvenile Orange lodges after a 2004 district meeting at Keta.

(of all types), and whilst this lessened after some years it had an impact on the Orange Order in Ghana. The country has since experienced the development of a well-rooted democracy, however. In 2000 and 2004, free and fair national elections were held, and the former opposition New Patriotic Party took and remains in power. Political problems are no longer regarded as problematic by the Orange leadership, who were positive about the organisation's future in this context.

A factor inhibiting recruitment was the rise of new charismatic churches, said to be popular because of their 'health and wealth' orientation. In conditions where people find it increasingly difficult to make ends meet and to understand why this should be so, spiritual explanations and spiritual solutions are offered. Seemingly undeserved poverty, lack of success and, conversely, power and wealth are often attributed to demonic activity. Many Ghanaians changed allegiance from old mission churches to these institutions that tend to preach against members' involvement in lodges of any type, which the churches regard as organisations harnessing occult powers for personal advancement. This message was supported by the flourishing 'Nollywood' video film industry, which has featured melodramas involving occult activity in wealthy men's lodge settings, such as *Billionaire's Club* (2003).

Chapter 16

'My father was a full-blooded Irishman': recollections of Irish immigrants in the 'slave narratives' from the New Deal's Works Progress Administration

Joe Regan

On 2 November 1938 Mal Boyd sat on his porch in Pine Bluff, Arkansas; he recollected his father's years as a slave in Texas: 'Papa belonged to Bill Boyd. Papa said he was his father and treated him just like the rest of his children. He said Bill Boyd was an Irishman. I know Papa looked kinda like an Irishman—face was red'.

Between 1936 and 1938, over 2,300 former American slaves from across seventeen different states were interviewed by the New Deal's Federal Writers' Project (FWP), a subset of the Works Progress Administration (WPA). As a part of the Second New Deal, President Franklin D. Roosevelt approved the establishment of the Works Progress Administration (WPA), which employed some five million Americans between 1934 and 1943. The Federal Writers' Project was established in 1935 as part of this to provide employment for teachers, writers, librarians and other unemployed white-collar workers. The aim of the project was to produce local histories and state guidebooks, and to record the recollections of ordinary Americans. This included former slaves. Amounting to over 10,000 typescript pages, the WPA's slave narratives comprise the largest single written source of US slaves' personal experiences. The WPA narratives provided surviving former slaves with an unparalleled opportunity to give their personal accounts of their experiences under the institution of slavery. Each narrative provides a microscopic representation of life in the different slave states of the South prior to emancipation. Although more than 70 years had elapsed between emancipation and the conducting of the interviews, these narratives also provide rich insights into white society and contain evidence of some slaves' interactions with Irish immigrants.

Slavery was the economic, social and political foundation of society in the Old South. Irish immigrants understood the potential of wealth generated from slave labour and that slave ownership served as the basis for elevated prestige and respect in southern society. Many Irish immigrants purchased slaves and

61. Litt Young from Texas, aged eighty-seven. He was a former slave of
    Martha Gibbs, 'a big, rich Irishwoman'. (Library of Congress)

some succeeded in becoming large planters. Although some Irishmen owned large plantations, thousands of other Irish immigrants laboured in the South. Southern whites, including Irish immigrants, often drank, gambled, stole, and slept with slaves and free blacks. The WPA narratives reveal a legacy of sexual relations between Irish men and female slaves.

It is important to note that the WPA slave narratives have generated considerable debate among American historians over their validity and legitimacy as reliable sources for understanding the experiences of the enslaved. For example, John W. Blassingame's *The slave community: plantation life in the antebellum South* (1972), an influential and pioneering work analysing the personal accounts of former slaves, deliberately omitted the WPA narratives, fearing that reliance on these accounts would provide 'a simplistic and distorted view of the plantations as a paternalistic institution where the chief feature of life was mutual love and respect between master and slave'. On the other hand, many recent historians, such as Mia Bay, Edward Baptist and Stephanie Camp, have argued the usefulness of the detailed observations recorded by the WPA narratives, and with careful reading they should not be discounted as a source.

Most of the informants had experienced slavery as young children, and many of those interviewed during the Depression years of the 1930s lived in abject poverty. In Tennessee, Maggie Broyles, whose father was 'a full-blood Irishman', admitted that she was 'having a hard time to scratch around and not go hungry'. The childhood experience of slavery and the hardship of the Great Depression were frequently compared, and many recalled their time in servitude favourably. For example, Ransom Sidney Taylor in Charlotte, North Carolina, provided an idyllic picture of plantation life and his former master, John Cane, 'an Irishman from the North'. Ransom recalled how 'mother and father said he was one o' the best white men that ever lived. I remember seein' him settin' on the porch in his large arm chair. He called me "Lonnie", a nickname. He called me a lot to brush off his shoes. I loved him he was so good.'

Cane's slaves always had 'plenty of something to eat' and Cane was portrayed as a benevolent master who 'would not allow anyone to whip his Negroes. If they were to be whipped he did it himself and the licks he gave them would not hurt a flea. He was good to all of us and we all loved him.' As children under the age of ten, many of the informants had not experienced at first hand the full rigours of plantation routine and discipline.

The WPA narratives included the testimony of an estimated 3% of former slaves still alive in the US. The representativeness of the accounts has been questioned owing to the disproportionate representation of information recorded. For example, Arkansas, which never had more than 3.5% of the US slave population, accounts for over 33% of the WPA's collected narratives. The most serious source of distortion in the narratives, however, came from the interviewers, the overwhelming majority of whom were white southern

62. and 63. 'In those days all the slaves had the religion of the master,' recalled
Donaville Broussard (left), a former French-speaking slave from
Louisiana. 'The priest came and held Mass for the white folks
sometimes.' Orelia Alexie Franks (right) was also raised 'where
everybody talk French'. She declared how 'I used to be a Catholic
but now I's a Apostolic'. (Library of Congress)

males. North Carolina, South Carolina and Alabama, for example, employed a total of one black interviewer, compared to Florida, which employed ten. The lack of black interviewers influenced the responses provided by the former slaves. During the 1930s, the Jim Crow system of racial segregation and white supremacy was securely entrenched and pervaded everyday life in the US South. Throughout this period, sharecropping and lynching demonstrated the nature of power in the South. White collectors often adopted patronising and condescending tones. Some informants mistook their interviewer for a government representative who might aid them economically and calculated their responses in an attempt to gain favour. For example, Josephine Stewart, aged 85, in Blackstock, South Carolina, concluded her interview with a plea, 'Please do all you can to get de good President, de Governor, or somebody to hasten up my old age pension dat I'm praying for'. Josephine's master's mother-in-law, 'Miss Anne Jane Neil', was 'a Irish lady, born in Ireland across de ocean'. A questionnaire was devised by John Lomax, National Advisor on Folklore for the WPA, but it was partially or completely ignored by the collectors. As a result, the quality of the accounts recorded is uneven and provides contradictory information about the nature of American slavery. The frankness of the much-quoted Martin Jackson of San Antonio, Texas, is not to be found in all accounts: 'Lots of old slaves closes the door before they tell the truth about their days of slavery. When the door is open, they tell how kind their master was and how rosy it all was.'

The slave narratives reveal that slaves encountered Irish immigrants at all levels of southern society, from planters to manual labourers. In Raleigh, North Carolina, former slave Charity Austin remembered how 'we children stole eggs and sold 'em durin' slavery. Some of de white men bought 'em. They were Irishmen and they would not tell on us.' In 1861 Angie Boyce was born into slavery in Kentucky. Her mother, Margaret King, attempted to reach her freed husband in Indiana. She was arrested, however, and placed in the Louisville jail and 'lodged in the same cell with [a] large brutal and drunken Irishwoman'. Enraged by the crying of Margaret's baby and 'crazed with drink', the Irishwoman threatened to 'bash its brains out against the wall if it did not stop crying'.

The interactions between slaves and Irish immigrants varied considerably, but those who laboured under an Irish overseer or were owned by an Irish master found that the latter could be just as ruthless as native-born white southerners. At the age of twelve Moses Mitchell was sold 'to an Irishman named John McInish in Marshall [Texas] for $1,500'. His mother and baby sister were left in Arkansas and he never saw either of them again. Investment in slavery was deemed economically prudent and the institution was avidly defended and morally justified by the various Christian churches in the US South, including the Catholic Church. Irish families consciously exploited and profited from the institution of slavery. Litt Young was a former slave of Martha Gibbs, 'a big,

64. President Franklin D. Roosevelt, pictured here about to broadcast one of his famous 'fireside chats'. As a part of the Second New Deal, he approved the establishment of the Works Progress Administration (WPA), which employed some five million Americans between 1934 and 1943. (Library of Congress)

rich Irishwoman and not scared of no man'. She enforced strict routines on her holdings outside Vicksburg, Mississippi. Young observed how his mistress 'buckled on two guns' before she went among the slaves and 'out-cussed a man when things didn't go right'. The work on Gibbs's plantation began when the 'big bell rung at four o'clock', with the overseer 'standin' there with a whippin' strap if you was late'. Cotton quotas were set for individual slaves and the 'last weighin' was done by lightin' a candle to see the scales'. Any picker 'not getting his task' got a whipping. Litt recalled how her second husband, Dr Gibbs, before the Civil War suggested to his wife that 'you oughtn't whip them black folks so hard'. Martha was quick to order her husband to 'shut up' and ignored his pleas. In 1863, after the fall of Vicksburg to Union forces, Martha Gibbs moved to Confederate-controlled Texas with her slaves. On their forced march Gibbs had hired Irishmen as guards, and Litt recalled that when they made camp at night 'they tied the men to trees. We couldn't git away with them Irishmen havin' rifles.' In Nashville, Tennessee, Emma Grisham remembered when the 'fightin' got so heavy mah white people got sum Irish people ter live on de plantation, en dey went south, leavin' us wid de Irish people'.

Wherever slaves worked on large plantations in the antebellum South, white men were typically hired as overseers to supervise and discipline the enslaved workforce. Among these were Irish overseers who undertook managerial positions on southern plantations. Violence was inherent in the plantation system, since it was the most successful method for slaveholders and overseers to resolve labour disputes. When an overseer failed to dominate the slaves, he failed to keep his job. Some overseers resorted to violence, sexual assault and the rape of slave women to assert their dominance and power. The sexual abuse of female slaves by overseers went largely unchecked. Most white men cared little for the consequences of their sexual relations with the slaves, but the children born from these relations left a lasting legacy. For example, in Woodward, South Carolina, John C. Brown stated that his wife Adeline Brown's father was 'a full blooded Irishman' who was the overseer for 'Marse Bob Clowney'. John divulged how the Irish overseer 'took a fancy for Adeline's mammy, a bright 'latto gal slave on de place. White women in them days looked down on overseers as poor white trash. Him couldn't git a white wife but made de best of it by puttin' in his spare time a-honeyin' 'round Adeline's mammy. Marse Bob stuck to him, and never 'jected to it.' The sexual abuse of slaves ranged from acts of punishment to forced reproduction and concubinage. Planters tolerated their overseers' sexual discrepancies, since they resulted in the birth of children like Adeline, a natural increase in the slaveholders' property. In Missouri, Betty Brown stated that her mother had five children before emancipation: 'Our daddy; he wuz an Irishman, name Millan, an' he had de bigges' [whiskey] still in all of Arkansas. Yes'm he had a white wife, an' five children at home, but mah mammy say he like huh an' she like him.' There were also some genuine relationships, which demonstrated kindness and affection between slaves and Irish immigrants. For example, Michael Morris Healy in Georgia was an Irish slaveholder who took extraordinary measures to secure the freedom of his slave children. In 1875 one of his sons, James Augustine Healy, became the Bishop of Portland, the first black Roman Catholic bishop ordained in the US.

The presence of black Irish Americans has received limited attention from historians of the Irish diaspora, and the WPA slave narratives are an important but neglected source for understanding the ambiguous relationship between the Irish and African Americans in the US. The evidence provided by the former slave narratives led one of the leading twentieth-century historians of the South, C. Vann Woodward, to remark that, given 'the mixture of sources and interpreters, interviewers and interviewees, the times and their "etiquette", the slave narratives can be mined for evidence to prove almost anything about slavery'. Just as the plantation records and the writings of planters cannot be used without caution, the slave narratives, like all primary sources, have their usefulness and limitations for understanding the past. The WPA slave narratives are too valuable to be left aside by historians and remain an important source for understanding American slavery. They also offer a new perspective on an under-studied part of the Irish story in America.

Bibliography

Akenson, Donald H., *The Irish Diaspora: A Primer* (Toronto, 1993)

Barnaby, Henry, 'The sack of Baltimore', *Journal of the Cork Historical and Archaeological Society* 74 (220) (July–December 1969), 101–129

Byrne, Cyril J (ed.), *Gentlemen-Bishops and Faction Fighters: The Letters of Bishops O Donel, Lambert, Scallan and other Irish Missionaries* (St John's 1984)

Delaney, Enda, *Irish Emigration since 1921* (Dublin, 2002)

Delaney, Enda 'Migration and Diaspora' in Jackson, Alvin (ed.), *The Oxford Handbook of Modern Irish History* (Oxford, 2014), 126-147

Doorley, Michael, *Irish-American Diaspora Nationalism: The Friends of Irish Freedom, 1916–1935* (Dublin, 2005)

Fitzgerald, Patrick and Lambkin, Brian, *Migration in Irish History, 1607-2007* (Basingstoke, 2008)

Fitzpatrick, David, *Irish Emigration, 1901-1921* (Dundalk, 1984)

Fitzpatrick, David, *Oceans of Consolation: Personal Accounts of Irish Migration to Australia* (Ithaca, NY, and Cork, 1994)

Harbison, Peter, *Pilgrimage in Ireland: The Monuments and the People* (London, 1991)

Hofstra, Warren R. (ed.), *Ulster to America: The Scots-Irish Migration Experience, 1680-1830* (Knoxville, 2012)

Jones, Maldwyn A., 'Scotch-Irish' in Thernstrom, Stephan (ed.), *Harvard Encyclopedia of American Ethnic Groups* (Cambridge, Mass, 1980), 895-908

Kenny, Kevin, *The American Irish: A History* (Harlow, 2000)

Kenny, Kevin (ed.), *Ireland and the British Empire* (Oxford, 2004)

Miller, Kerby A., *Emigrants and Exiles: Ireland and the Irish Exodus to North America* (NY and Oxford 1985)

Miller, Kerby A, Schrier, Arnold, Boling, Bruce D. and Doyle, David N. (eds.), *Irish Immigrants in the Land of Canaan* (Oxford and New York, 2003)

McClintock, H.F. *Old Irish and Highland Dress* (Dundalk, 1949)

O'Connor, Thomas (ed.), *The Irish in Europe, 1580-1815* (Dublin, 2001)

O'Farrell, Patrick (ed.), *Letters from Irish Australia, 1825–1929* (Sydney and Belfast, 1984)

Rodgers, Nini, *Ireland, Slavery and Anti-Slavery, 1612–1865* (Basingstoke, 2007)

Hereward, *The Fenians and Canada* (Toronto, 1978)

Sherling, Rankin, *The Invisible Irish: Finding Protestants in the Nineteenth-Century Migrations to America* (Montreal and Kingston, 2016)

Stalley, Roger, 'Sailing to Santiago: medieval pilgrimage to Santiago de Compostela and its artistic influence in Ireland', in Bradley, John (ed.), *Settlement and Society in the Middle Ages* (Kilkenny, 1988), 397–420

Walsh, Barbara, *Roman Catholic Nuns in England and Wales 1800–1937: A Social History* (Dublin and Portland, 2002)

Wilson, David A., *Thomas D'Arcy McGee, vol. I: Passion, Reason and Politics, 1825–57* (Montreal and Kingston, 2008)